THE ALTERNATIV

Rescued from oblivion, the T'ai Hsüan Ching, a
to the I Ching, is now presented in English for the first time.

Wen Wang, 1231-1135 BC, founder of the Chou Dynasty, and father of Wu Wang, its first ruler. During his imprisonment under the Yin dynasty, Wen Wang occupied his two years in compiling an arrangement of the symbols of the Book of Changes.

THE ALTERNATIVE I CHING

by

Derek Walters

THE AQUARIAN PRESS
Wellingborough, Northamptonshire

First published as *The T'ai Hsüan Ching*, 1983
This Edition first published 1987

For Matthew Franklin

British Library Cataloguing in Publication Data

Walters, Derek
[The t'ai hsüan ching]. The alternative
I Ching
1. Divination — China
I. The t'ai hsüan ching II. Title
III. Yang, Xiong. Tai xuan jing.
133.3'0951 BF1773.2.C5

ISBN 0-85030-659-0

The Aquarian Press is part of the Thorsons Publishing Group, Wellingborough, Northamptonshire, NN8 2RQ, England

Printed in Great Britain by Woolnough Bookbinding,
Irthlingborough, Northamptonshire

2 4 6 8 10 9 7 5 3

CONTENTS

The 81 Tetragrams, arranged in *T'ien*.

INTRODUCTION

The T'ai Hsüan Ching is an ancient book of divination embodying ideas with far-reaching implications for mathematics and science even today. Although it was assembled by the philosopher Yang Hsiung two thousand years ago, it has remained in obscurity simply because its extraordinary qualities have been understood by only a few perspicacious scholars. Indeed, its apparent resemblance to the I Ching has been the major cause of the work's not having been made known to a wider readership, with those in a position to disseminate the teachings of this classic all too readily dismissing it as a pastiche of little literary value. Its detractors have therefore overlooked several vital points. To begin with, the T'ai Hsüan Ching is principally a book of divination, and secondly a work of philosophy. Neither Nostradamus nor Newton is read for his literary value. Thirdly, the compiler, Yang Hsiung, declared that he set himself quite different standards to those that were accepted as the literary criteria of his time. 'What is to be esteemed in a writer,' he wrote, in a passage quoted by Feng Yu Lan, in '*A History of Chinese Philosophy*' 'is his conforming to, and the embodiment of, spontaneity . . . Therefore he neither discards what is possessed by spontaneity, nor strains after what it lacks. The case is like the body; adding to it causes excrescence; taking away causes injury'.

Next, another point which seems to have been missed is that the I Ching was neither the only, nor even the first, method of divination which involved diagrams of lines. Nor was the system confined to China. Rhabdomancy (casting rods, by which the diagrams of the I Ching are calculated) was known to the Greeks as a Scythian practice, suggesting that the art may have been introduced into China by Mongol seers; on the other hand, '*Napoleon's Book of Fate*' which uses similar diagrams claims to have Ancient Egyptian origins. Two other methods of divination, similar to the I Ching, are mentioned in classical literature: these are the Lien Shan (Mountain Chains) attributed to Fu Hsi the legendary sage, and the Kuei Tsang (Return to the Life Source) attributed to the equally legendary Yellow Emperor, (Shang) Huang Ti. Furthermore, there is now considerable archaeological evidence which suggests that most tribes had their own seers, who practised their own systems of divination, using not six lines but four, five, and perhaps eight.

Of these many different methods, the 'I Ching' is the only work which bears the title 'Changes'. Thus, the 'Book of Changes' implies that the other divinatory systems were *not* 'books of changes' at all, though the alternative title, the 'Chou I' meaning the 'Changes of the Chou (Dynasty)' suggests that there could have been another book of changes, perhaps of the Han dynasty at the latest, or Shang at the earliest. The discovery of documents at present being examined in China may prove this to be the actual case. As a consequence, the pertinent factor about the I Ching which set it apart from other works lay in the system of 'changing' hexagrams.

Critics who maintain that the T'ai Hsüan Ching is merely a pale imitation of the I Ching, unaccountably overlook several defects of the 'I Ching'. The texts of the sixty-four hexagrams (discounting the 'commentaries' added by later hands) are an assembly of heterogenous phrases which range from magic formulae (the first hexagram notably and many others later) to complete poems (as in the Song of the Well, hexagram 48). Many of them repeat whole portions of the texts of other hexagrams. The order of the hexagrams is also an apparently random one (at least, no-one has yet convincingly explained the reason for the sequence). On the other hand, the T'ai Hsüan Ching is an extremely sophisticated work; the order of the diagrams follows a logical sequence; there is a unifying philosophy linking the sequence together, and the texts, as diverse and as varied as they are, are nevertheless assembled with care. The I Ching is a random collection of folk-sayings, which have become frozen into a complete work before maturity; the T'ai Hsüan Ching is so much more cohesive that it cannot really be compared with the earlier work. But the main misunderstanding lies in neglecting the inherent philosophy of the T'ai Hsüan Ching. Briefly, the T'ai Hsüan Ching holds that there are three forces at work in nature; two of these, the Yin and the Yang, represent the positive and negative fluxes of electro-magnetism; but there is also a third force which accounts for the creation of the truly novel. With Yin and Yang there is nothing new under the Sun. While everything can be classified as belonging to Yin and Yang, the dual philosophy can only account for what exists already; no matter what resultant products or ideas are spawned by the action of Yin and Yang, there is no entirely new element created. The results of any action can be foretold by the component materials and forces. But new ideas, and new species, only arise from the action of the third creative force. It is well known that an electronic computer can only produce what is fed into it; it takes the human mind to generate new concepts. The third force, according to the T'ai Hsüan Ching, is the Jen (Mankind) force. The full implications of this radical theory are discussed in the chapter on 'The T'ai Hsüan Ching and Scientific Thought'. Thus, far from being 'based on the I Ching' the T'ai Hsüan Ching (in its four-lined diagrams) draws upon sources much older than extant versions of the I Ching; the philosophy of the triad is totally at variance with the duality of the I Ching, and yet, paradoxically as though it might seem, the T'ai Hsüan Ching is a work of tremendous originality.

Finally, to the T'ai Hsüan's use as a vehicle of divination. The I Ching has attracted the attentions of three thousand years of devoted study. The T'ai Hsüan Ching, though it has appeared in several editions, and has counted many eminent Chinese scholars among its apologists, has languished in neglect for two thousand of those years. Only a couple of passages have ever been translated from the Chinese into any other language, one of these being Russian. Against the massive collection of some two hundred volumes of *selected* classical writings of the I Ching must be set the handful of paragraphs on the T'ai Hsüan Ching written by a few specialists. Yet, the few people who have had the opportunity to approach the T'ai Hsüan Ching have been astonished by the book's extraordinary ability to relate to the questioner, far more directly and much more materially than the abstruse comments of the I Ching. It is hoped that the further research needed to assess this aspect of a most remarkable work may now become possible with the availability of this text.

Divination Systems Related to the T'ai Hsüan Ching

In classical times the familiar I Ching was only one of three books on divination which formed the Grand Oracle, Ta Pu (大卜). The others were the Lien Shan (連山) Mountain Chains, and the Kuei Tsang (歸藏) Return to the Life Source, attributed to the equally legendary Yellow Emperor, (Shang) Huang Ti. These two works have long been presumed lost, supposedly destroyed in the great 'Burning of the Books' carried out by another 'Yellow Emperor' Shih Huang Ti, in 213 BC.

The Book of the Rites of Chou asserts that these two books were similar in many respects to the I Ching; it is therefore necessary to recapitulate briefly the nature of the I Ching. It is a most complex book, concerned with the interpretations of 64 diagrams, each of which consists of six lines, either broken or unbroken. Each diagram has a title name; this is followed by a short text, a commentary, and then an interpretation of each of the lines of the text. The basic text of the I Ching is that which immediately follows the diagram; though undoubtedly the most ancient, it is extremely heterogenous, and may vary from one or two characters which merely indicate good or bad fortune, to a verse of some almost-forgotten significance: magic charms, prayers, or a snatch of an ancient rhyme. The commentaries, interpretations, and division into lines are generally agreed to be the work of Wen Wang and his son Chou Kung, (died 1105 BC) founder of the Chou dynasty.

There are two possible solutions which might explain the disappearance of the Lien Shan and the Kuei Tsang. To begin with, it would be in contradiction of the known facts if they were regarded as having been destroyed in the Burning of the Books, since Shih Huang Ti specifically spared 'practical' books, such as those on divination, and incidentally, including the I Ching. The likelihood is therefore that they were not destroyed or lost, but were gathered up among the texts of the other works; or alternatively, that the titles were not names of books at all, but *methods* of divination. For example, the diagrams of the I Ching are selected by a process which involves dividing a bundle of yarrow stalks (why yarrow stalks is explained in a later chapter; see page 51, and observing the remainders after such divisions. In the I Ching, the significant remainders are 6 and 9. It is possible that other methods may have used an alternative selection process, resulting in different remainder, such as 7 and 8 (see the article by Zhang Zhenglang, referred to below). Alternatively, the order of the diagrams, and their allocation to certain oracular verses, may have varied. For example, traditionally the I Ching begins with the diagrams ䷀ Ch'ien (Heaven, dry, male 乾) and K'un (Earth, wet, female 坤). But recent archaeological discoveries have unearthed fragments of a text of the I Ching in which the first symbol is 鍵 Chien (a door-bolt) and the second is Ch'uan (巛), a Stream, which represents not just a different order of characters, but different titles altogether for the diagrams. A suggestion made by Zhang Zhenglang (*Kaogu Xuebao*, 1980, No 4) is that each tribe had its own system of divination, which it practised before founding a city; and that the name of the tribe became associated with both the means of the divination and the name of the city.

It is generally accepted that even older than the I Ching is the more elementary system of Eight Diagrams (Pa Kua), also attributed to the mystic Fu Hsi. These eight diagrams (which have now become almost synonymous with the points of the compass, as well as a required part of every Chinese talisman) are supposed to have originated at some distant time in history in company with another mystic diagram, the Lo Shu, or River Picture, an arrangement of the numbers 1 to 9 in a mathematical magic square. (See page 46.) We shall see shortly another connection between the mystic nine numbers and the diagrams of broken lines.

Apart from the six-line diagrams of the I Ching (hexagrams) and the eight three-line diagrams of the Pa Kua, there are some very similar curious markings on oracle bones (the most ancient Chinese texts), ceremonial bronzes, and other artefacts. These are diagrams of four lines, broken into twos and threes. Various meanings have been attributed to these diagrams, and it has been suggested that they may have been a primitive form of numbering, or date.

Examples of such 'strange signs' on oracle bones are illustrated in *Kaogu* (Archaeology) No. 2, 1981. Examples on bronzes are described in an article by B. Schindler in *Ostasiatische Zeitschrift*, 1915, vol. 3. Further evidence that the signs were divinatory is given in a later article on bronzes to be found in the English language *The Wonder of Chinese Bronzes* by Li Xueqin, who mentions that Shang and Chou dynasty bronze vessels, such as the ones found at Chou Yuan in the Shanhsi province, had engraved numbers which were reminiscent of the signs found on oracle bones. The numbers on these bronzes are grouped in threes and sixes, but limited to the digits 1, 5, 6, 7 and 8. The inference is that these numbers were the result of divinations, but it is difficult to see how the bronzes were so used.

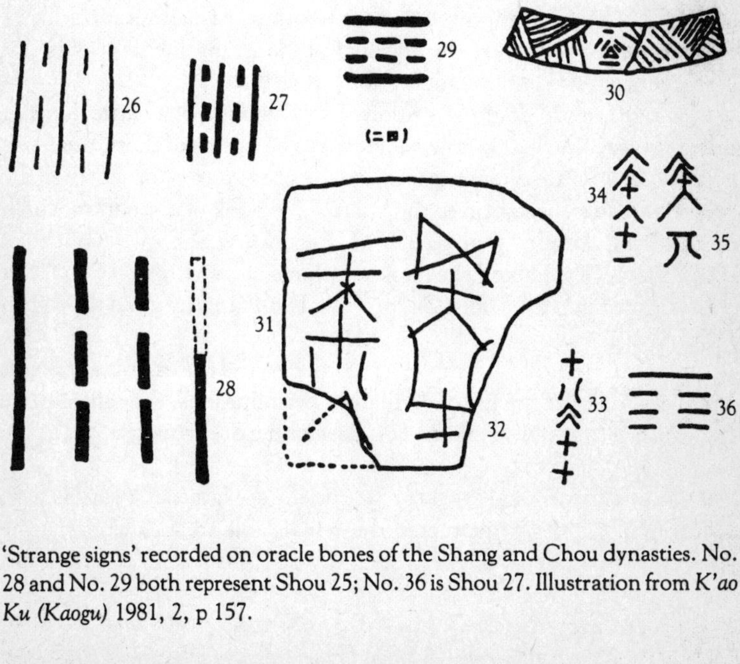

'Strange signs' recorded on oracle bones of the Shang and Chou dynasties. No. 28 and No. 29 both represent Shou 25; No. 36 is Shou 27. Illustration from *K'ao Ku (Kaogu)* 1981, 2, p 157.

From a totally different source are the wood-cut symbols recorded by the pioneering Schlagintweit brothers on one of their incursions into the Himalayas in the mid-nineteenth century. These last Sikkimese signs, however, whatever their dates and provenance, resemble neither the eight 'Kua' of the I Ching nor the eighty-one Shou of the T'ai Hsüan Ching, but instead have curious vertical markings in addition to the horizontal lines, and are quite unlike any Chinese signs ever recorded. They could, of course, refer to a different method of divination yet again.

Whether these symbols are dates, or divination symbols akin to those of the I Ching and the Pa Kua, then there would be a total possibility of 81 such diagrams. This is a significant figure, for frequently in divination texts one runs against the notion of a Mystic Square of numbers, arranged in a grid, 9×9. Once certain calculations had been effected, reference was made to the grid to find the appropriate divination title. Such a table exists — The Tsan Chiu Feng Pa Shih I Ming Shu, although it is deficient, showing but 71 out of the possible 81 titles.

Foı the sake of completeness, another work of divination which might at first glance appear to be related, is the Ling Ch'i Ching, or Manual of Spirit Chess. In this, there were twelve pieces bearing the characters for Top, Middle, and Bottom; four of each category. These would seem to equate to the lines of the mysterious tetragrams, since there are four lines in each tetragram, each capable of division into one, two or three. The Ling Ch'i Ching, however, does not have 81 permutations in its divination, but 120, which include not just the arrangements of all twelve pieces, but all the lesser combinations as well.

The solution of a doubt was resolved by the result of a battle. It is not fully understood whether this was meant to be a game of chess, the result of a physical battle of animated magnetic chess pieces, or whether the pieces were merely cast on to the board. The book of divination which revealed the portents is attributed to T'ung Fang Shuo, a favourite of the Emperor Wu Ti, and the book may have been written in 113 BC. It was absorbed into the Taoist Canon (The Tao Tsang) in about the eighth century AD.

Whatever method was employed to operate the pieces, it is apparent, from looking over the list of divinatory permutations, that all or none of the pieces may have remained on the gaming or divining board at the end of the operation.

It is now only necessary to introduce briefly the fact that Yang Hsiung, a Han philosopher, constructed the remarkable treatise which is the subject of this book, and to say that it is based on a system of tetragrams and a grid 9×9.

The following table shows the correspondences, or otherwise, between all the divination titles which have been described above.

Magic charm from Sikkim

It is difficult to ascertain from the woodcut whether the diagrams depicted are meant to be white on black, or black on white. If they are meant to be white on black, then they are trigrams, like the Eight Diagrams, but with the following differences. The usual order of the Eight Diagrams is as follows:

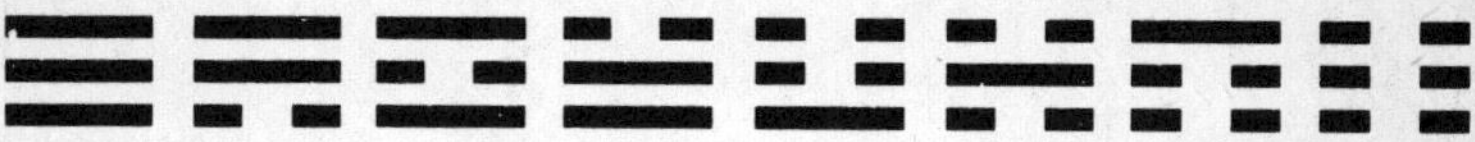

1 2 3 4 5 6 7 8

The order of the diagrams in the Sikkimese sequence would appear to be 7 2 7 6 1 4 8 3. In this case, Kua 5 is missing. However, the two Kua 7 do not appear to be the same character. In the first of the Kua shown, the two lower lines are broken, but do not have the extra black division shown in the third Kua. There is a distinct difference in the breaking of the central white line in the eighth Kua, for example, and the breaking of the line of the sixth Kua. It is quite clear that if they are white on black, there is a vertical joining of the lines. Yet the same puzzle applies if it is supposed that the lines are black on a white background, thus forming eight tetragrams of four lines each. Reversing the colours, this is how the four-lined tetragrams would appear:

It is still necessary to account for the difference between the bottom half of the second symbol and the bottom half of the fourth symbol. It cannot be that the presence of a joining vertical line simply indicates the division of a line into three, since this still does not explain the difference between diagrams 4 and 7. More likely, they represent a different system altogether.

Character	Magic Square	T'ai Hsüan	I Ching
閑	7	4	—
蒙	6	—	4
戾	47	6	—
訟	62	—	6
比	28	—	8
交	22	16	—
隨	80	—	17
從	21	19	—
親	17	34	—
射	24	—	34
晉	30	—	35
夷	—	23	36

Character	Magic Square	T'ai Hsüan	I Ching
損	50	—	41
遇	74	43	—
益	32	—	42
萃	18	—	45
革	68	—	49
常	14	51	—
守	3	57	—
節	46	61	—
止	70	71	—
堅	67	72	—
養	73	81	—

Table of Correspondences between the I Ching, the T'ai Hsüan Ching, and the Magic Tablet of Eighty-One Squares.

All the characters contained in the titles of the Ling Ch'i Ching, the T'ai Hsüan Ching, the I Ching, the Magic Tablet of Eighty-One Squares, and the aspects of the nine numbers of the Lo Shu were indexed to see if there were any correlations between the various systems. One of the difficulties was that the Ling Ch'i Ching titles, taken from two sources (see bibliography) had variations in the names of the titles, each of which consisted of two characters. The titles of the T'ai Hsüan Ching uniformly consist of one character, as do the titles of the Eighty-One Magic Squares, though of course since the latter is incomplete, it is not possible to determine whether any of the missing titles may have had two characters. The I Ching consists mainly of single character titles, although a few have double characters; in the latter case, the auxilliary character is usually nothing more than an adjective, e.g. 'Great' or 'Small'. In the Ling Ch'i Ching, not only are the names of the titles subject to variation, but in other cases the characters may be in reverse order. There seemed to be no apparent consistency in these variations. Because of the problems involved; from which no definite conclusions could be drawn, the Ling Ch'i Ching, with its catalogue of some 300 title characters, has been left out of this list.

養 73	寬 64	迅 55	飾 46	37	比 28	見 19	成 10	原 1
遇 74	賓 65	懼 56	戾 47	38	開 29	獲 20	沖 11	潛 2
勝 75	危 66	除 57	虛 48	39	晉 30	從 21	振 12	守 3
凶 76	堅 67	弱 58	昧 49	40	公 31	交 22	析 13	信 4
壬 77	革 68	疾 59	損 50	41	益 32	育 23	常 14	直 5
固 78	報 69	競 60	用 51	42	章 33	壯 24	矛 15	蒙 6
移 79	止 70	分 61	卻 52	43	盈 34	興 25	易 16	閑 7
隨 80	戎 71	訟 62	翁 53	44	35	欣 26	親 17	須 8
終 81	結 72	收 63	遠 54	寡 45	36	舒 27	萃 18	厲 9

The 9×9 Magic Square of 81 Fates.

The Magic Square of Master Tsan (Tortoise) is closely related to the arrangement of the T'ai Hsüan Ching. The numbering system was the one in use during the Han dynasty, and about a hundred years either side. Ten of the characters are the same as the titles of the I Ching hexagrams, and two of them, squares 48 and 66, are the astrological signs 11 and 12 of the lunar mansions. Four of them are the same as the titles of the T'ai Hsüan Ching, but there are no exact correspondences. Square 73, which heads the final *T'ien* of the T'ai Hsüan Ching, is occupied by the character Yang, Shou 81 in the T'ai Hsüan Ching; the closest correspondence is perhaps that of square 70, equivalent to Shou 71. (The 81 squares can be seen in their entirety in the Appendix page 210ff.)

PART ONE:
THE T'AI HSÜAN CHING

INTRODUCTION TO THE T'AI HSÜAN CHING

The text of the T'ai Hsüan Ching is divided into 81 sections known as Shou (首), or 'chiefs'. These 81 Shou are numbered by means of a system of four-lined diagrams, conveniently called 'tetragrams' (analogous to the term 'hexagram' used for the six-lined diagrams of the I Ching). These tetragrams follow a logical mathematical sequence, according to a ternary system of numerical notation. These four lines have their own technical terminology as follows:

The top, principal line:	Fang	(方)	A square, direction, or compass point.
The second line:	Chou	(州)	A division.
The third line:	Pu	(部)	A department.
The fourth (bottom) line:	Chia	(家)	A family.

Each of these lines may be whole, or divided into two, or three parts. In the sequence, the first Shou has four unbroken lines, the second Shou has the bottom line divided into two, the third Shou the bottom line divided into three; the fourth Shou has the Pu line divided into two but with the Chia line whole. The sequence continues in regular order, ending with Shou 81, in which all four lines are divided into three. (A cursory glance at the illustration on page 6 will make this quite clear.) The first four tetragrams therefore appear as follows:

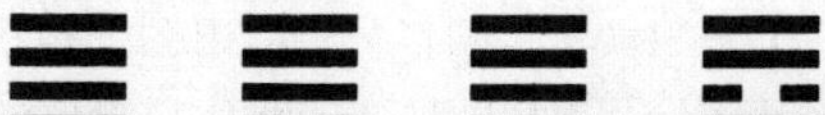

1 2 3 4

On this topic, it is worthwhile pointing out that the order of the 64 hexagrams of the I Ching, in their present form, does not follow a logical sequence. Hexagram 1, Ch'ien, which consists of six unbroken lines, is followed immediately by Hexagram 2, K'un, consisting of six broken lines.

Similarly, the rest of the hexagrams are all arranged in pairs, not following any mathematical rule. If the hexagrams were laid out as a sequence of binary numbers, thus:

they would be numbers 1, 44, 13 and 33.

Now it is well-known, among I Ching students, that there are two arrangements of the eight 'trigrams' from which the hexagrams were derived; the Fu Hsi arrangement, and the 'modern' arrangement (at least a thousand years old) attributed to Wen Wang, who is also credited with arranging the 64 hexagrams in their present order. The Fu Hsi arrangement of the trigrams *does* follow a mathematical sequence; it is not too far-fetched to think that the original arrangement of the 64 hexagrams also followed a binary sequence, as shown above. Recent excavations and the discovery of more ancient texts of the I Ching have shed new light on this problem.

These 81 Shou have names, or titles, to identify them, in addition to the numbering system above. They are classified into three groups, numbers 1-27 being regarded as Yang; the middle group, numbers 28-54, being regarded as a mixture of Yang and Yin; and a third group, numbers 55-81, which are considered to be Yin. These three groupings are called T'ien, Heaven, (Nos. 1-27); Jen, Man, (Nos. 28-54); and Ti, Earth, (Nos. 55-81).

The 81 Shou are also divided into 9 equal divisions, each of which, unfortunately somewhat confusingly, is also called *T'ien**. These nine *T'ien* are the groups 1-9, 10-18, 19-27, and so on. The first three *T'ien* (just enumerated) therefore form the larger group known as T'ien, while the fourth, fifth, and sixth *T'ien* form the group Jen. Similarly, the last three *T'ien* form the Ti, Earth group, i.e., Shou 55-81.

These nine *T'ien* take their names from the first Shou in the group. Hence the *T'ien* which consists of Shou 1-9 is known as Chung, since Chung is the name of Shou 1. Similarly, Shou 10, Hsien, gives its name to the *T'ien* containing 10-18.

According to Yang Hsiung, each of the Shou was *capable* of being divided into nine further sub-divisions, called Tsan (assistants) making 729 Tsan in all. Most editions of the T'ai Hsüan Ching (except the edition by Ch'en Jen Hsi, upon which the present work is based) actually show these 729 Tsan, and even have commentaries on the text; but as will be

* To lessen the confusion, the word *T'ien*, when meaning a sub-division, will be written in italics.

shown later, it is not certain that these Tsan texts are actually by Yang Hsiung; the likelihood is that they are not. All that can be said for any specific Tsan number is that its interpretation must lie within a definite Shou: Tsan 365, for example, must belong to Shou 41; but which particular part of that text actually applies to Tsan 365 must be open to conjecture. A list of the Tsan, and the *T'ien* and Shou to which they belong, is given in the table *To Find the T'ien and Shou'* on page 42.

The Content of the Shou Texts

The Shou texts are a curious mixture of the deeply philosophical and the domestically banal; the romantically poetic and the tritely mundane; the clear and the abstruse.

As has been mentioned already, each Shou has a name, or title character. This character may occur once or more times during the course of the text; or it may not appear at all. In the latter case, however (as in Shou 39, a Dwelling), there is usually some correlation between the title of the Shou and the content of the text. Many of the Shou, and virtually all the first forty, then commence with an opening formula regarding the Yin or Yang nature of the Shou. Nearly all the first forty texts begin Yang Ch'i (陽氣) here translated as 'active flux'. Since this appears to be a standard opening formula, it follows that in translating the rest of the text these two characters ought to be disregarded. This is vitally important, for if the opening verse is taken out of context with this standard formula attached to it, the meaning of the whole phrase could be changed. This in fact is exactly what has happened in the case of the quotation which appears in Giles' Dictionary (see the commentary to Shou 3).

Following the opening Yang or Yin formula, there is frequently a line or two which expands on the nature of the 'Yin' and 'Yang' which pertain to that particular Shou; for example, in Shou 35:

> *'Active flux:*
> *Great self-sufficiency on the outside;*
> *Modicum of Yin:*
> *A little accumulation on the inside.'*

A continuation of this 'philosophical' statement is the 'elemental' nature of the Shou. (The term 'element' as used in the text is explained elsewhere; see page 32). For example '*A frontier inside, unyielding outside*' (Shou 29). These philosophical texts are now always at the beginning of the Shou; they may appear anywhere during the course of the text. Shou 81 is exceptional in having an additional philosophical verse at the end, which very neatly brings the whole Shou, and indeed the entire text, to an elegant conclusion.

Some of these philosophical statements are remarkable in the extreme; they seem to indicate that Yang Hsiung's grasp of the natural sciences was far ahead of his time. What are we to make of such statements as '*Since flight alters the appearance of things, the transformation of objects can be made by the intellect*' (Shou 28) which almost suggests the FitzGerald-Lorentz contraction phenomenon of the Theory of Relativity? And what can we make of his assertion that '*Plants are the central pivot without which the world outside would gasp for breath*'? Was Yang Hsiung aware that without plants, there would be no oxygen, and we would be unable to breathe?

Another kind of statement which appears early on in the text to the Shou is the 'almanac' or 'calendrical' indication. (The relationship between the T'ai Hsüan Ching and the calendar is dealt with more fully on pages 33ff). One type is a kind of nature diary for the year, as in '*Hatching tiny things each crafty pair*' (Shou 6) or '*twigs and branches emerging*' (Shou 15). The other type deals with astronomical phenomena, or the basic administration of the calendar (see Shou 37, 41, and 67) which corroborate the suggestions outlined in these pages for the correlation of the T'ai Hsüan Ching with the Western calendar.

Then there are social and domestic statements '*Taxes are manacles*' (Shou 21), '*We defer to authority and show respect*' (Shou 9) '*The Knight* [or cultured person] *yields to his neighbours*' (Shou 25), and numerous references to domestic life; sitting round the stove, taking tea, and discussions about marriage. There are doctors and quacks (Shou 51 and 75), references to travel by carriage and boat; mythical beasts, farmyard animals, and a veritable aviary of birds of a type unknown to me. These are the sybilline verses; the omens which should be considered deeply, and interpreted in the light of the questioner's problems.

Some of these oracle verses may appear to be quite unrelated to the rest of the text, and certainly to the title of the Shou itself. In Shou 45 the word Li (a sacrificial vessel) appears, totally unrelated to anything which has gone before; even the verse which follows is unrelated, either to the rest of the Shou, or to the word Li. Consisting of only one character, it is one of the shortest verses in the whole of the T'ai Hsüan Ching (it is not unique in being a single character verse, although it is remarkable in being totally unrelated to the context).

It is possible that some of these 'inspirational' verses were generated by the actual form of other characters in the text, producing a 'stream of consciousness' kind of writing that was ideal for the creation of mysterious, dream-like images among a mesh of tight, philosophical argument. Shou 36 and 56 are possible illustrations of this kind of writing.

A feature of the poetic style is the contrasting of pairs of verses which may begin with either identical statements, or contradictory ones.

> '*Inside, there is clarity;*
> *There is no need for a light.*
> *Inside, there is clarity;*
> *The Self is deep, yet explored.*' (Shou 63)

is an example of the first kind of 'contrasting verse', while the following is a 'contradictory' one.

> '*There is no increase;*
> *It is the Direction.*
> *There is increase;*
> *It is light in the darkness.*' (Shou 13).

Allied with the foregoing is the self-contradictory statement, 'A is not A' or paradox. The ancient scholars delighted in such intriguing riddles: some forty-odd paradoxes are listed in Joseph Needham's *Science and Civilisation in China:* Volume II pp. 190-192. They date from the fourth century BC, so the notion of a paradoxical statement would not be new to Yang Hsiung. In the T'ai Hsüan Ching we read, for example, '*Yellow is not yellow*', (Shou 1), '*poverty is not poverty*' (Shou 5), and '*contention is not contention*', (Shou 25).

There is no set formula or pattern for the Shou texts as a whole, although there is the occasional 'model' text which embodies many of the elements discussed above — Shou 13 is a good example, since it begins with the Yang Ch'i formula, followed by an almanac statement '*Luxuriant growth increasing*' and a number of oracular verses, two of which have already been quoted. Some of the Shou consist entirely of philosophical statements, Shou 73 being one of the most remarkable. Others, for example Shou 76, are entirely oracular, the last mentioned being of particular interest since the text does not include the 'title' character, which is nevertheless suggested by its component parts.

It is hoped that the commentaries on these texts will help to unravel some of the mysteries of what are at first reading extremely obscure texts. They are, nonetheless, extremely deep, and continue to reveal a profundity of ideas '*hoarded in the heart of the abyss*'. I leave that quotation from the T'ai Hsüan Ching for the reader to find!

Yang Hsiung: A Biographical Sketch

The compiler of the T'ai Hsüan Ching, Yang Hsiung (titled Tse Yün) was born about 53BC, a time when Julius Caesar was planning his invasion of Britain, at the other side of the known world. Most of what is known about Yang Hsiung comes from an account of his life by the Han dynasty historian, Pan Ku, (a great admirer of Yang Hsiung) whose comments on the T'ai Hsüan Ching are quoted by Ch'en Jen Hsi in the preface to his edition of the T'ai Hsüan Ching (that is, the edition on which the present version is based).

According to Pan Ku (who lived from AD32-92) Yang Hsiung was born in P'i Hsien, a district of Cheng Tu, the capital of Sze-chuan. His family name was derived from the township of Yang Hsien, in Shansi, which was formerly held in fief by one of the philosopher's ancestors. However, by the time Yang Hsiung was born, the family were in somewhat reduced circumstances; indeed, they were to remain so, for even at the height of Yang Hsiung's career, the family never had more than a few gold pieces between them. But this nigh-poverty never troubled Yang Hsiung, who was more concerned in following his scholarly pursuits than in acquiring material possessions. Even as a child, he was known for the thoroughness with which he pursued his studies, not being content with learning his lessons parrot-fashion, but instead striving to grasp the meaning of obscure passages by studying the whole context.

An impediment prevented his being a good speaker — perhaps being cut off from society by his inability to converse readily prompted him to withdraw into a more cloistered, academic life — there may be a hint of this in Shou 56 for example 'The mouth clamours, gabbling; humming lacks speech'. Humming, in this context, could mean a striving to speak.

About 13BC, he went to Chang An, and was appointed to the equivalent of an assistant lectureship at a university. Later, he became secretary to the Censor's office. Then occurred an event which was to have several impacts on Yang Hsiung's life and work, and even on the way in which his works were to be received by posterity. It is very likely that the reason why Yang Hsiung's philosophies have remained in obscurity is the reception that they received by later critics, not for their content, but for political attitudes towards Yang Hsiung's tenure of a post under a rebel emperor. And yet this attitude was totally unjustified. The Han dynasty fell in AD9 to the Regent, Meng, and Yang Hsiung was actually arrested and implicated in a plot to overthrow the rebel. Waiting trial, he fled by jumping from the window of the tower in which he was imprisoned, and must have been seriously injured, since it is recorded that he almost lost his life.

However, he evidently managed to exonerate himself, because later he was appointed to the post of Ta Fu (Great Scholar). This may have been for his earlier writings, which had praised Meng before he usurped the throne. Other historians however, regarded these panegyrics as evidence of treasonous behaviour (despite the fact that they were composed before the revolution, as courtesy odes) and unbefitting for a moral philosopher. This led to his writings being regarded with some disfavour, and consequently they were less circulated, and less widely appreciated, than they might have been.

Besides the T'ai Hsüan Ching, he was the compiler of a dialect dictionary, a book on music, and other writings which unfortunately have been lost. By far the most widely celebrated of his writings is the *Fa Yen*, a collection of pithy sayings after the style of the Lun Yu (The Conversations and Discourses of Confucius — *the 'Analects'*). Until now, the T'ai Hsüan Ching has remained as obscure as its title would suggest, referred to only by academics for its curiosity value, and seldom studied.

His official biography states that he died in AD18, aged 71.

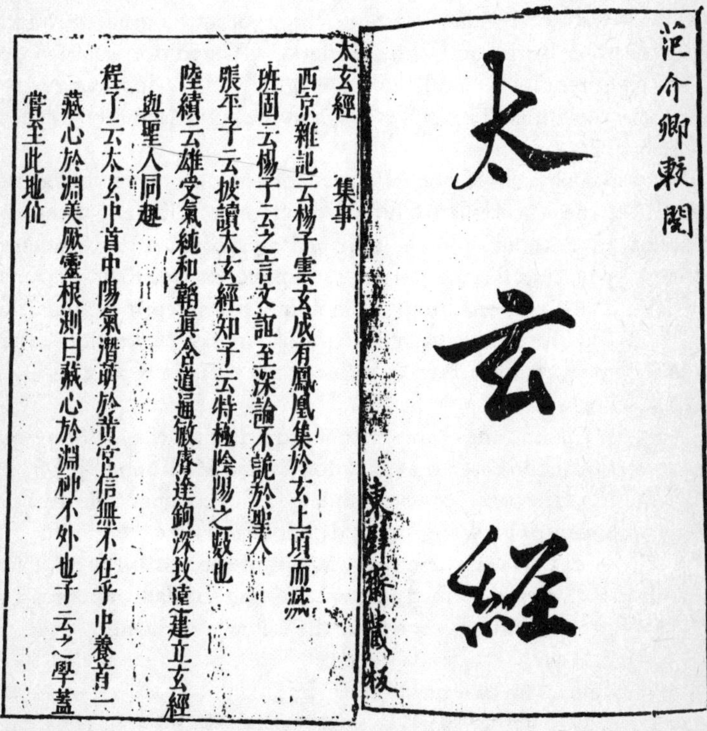
范介卿較閲
太玄經
東壁齋藏板

太玄經 集事
西京雜記云楊子雲玄成有鳳凰集於玄上頃而滅
班固云楊子云之言文誼至深論不詭於聖人
張平子云披讀太玄經知子云特極陰陽之數也
陸績云雄受氣純和韜真含道通敏叡達鉤深致遠建立玄經
與聖人同趣
程子云太玄中首中陽氣潛萌於黃宮信無不在乎中養首一
藏心於淵美厥靈根測曰藏心於淵神不外也子云之學蓋
嘗至此地位

The title page of Ch'en Jen Hsi's edition of the T'ai Hsüan Ching, with comments by eminent Chinese classical scholars.

EXTANT VERSIONS OF THE T'AI HSÜAN CHING

The text on which this English version of the T'ai Hsüan Ching has been based is that of an old woodcut book, bound with some other contemporary pamphlets, in the Department of Oriental Manuscripts and Printed Books in the British Library, London. The date, DCCXV pencilled on the cover of the collection shows that they must have come into the possession of some Western scholar or antiquarian very early in the history of British and Chinese relations. The edition was prepared by the great scholar Ch'en Jen Hsi (陳仁錫), 1579-1634, one of the officials of the Imperial Examination, and the compiler of the Imperial Encyclopaedia.

This particular text is of especial interest for a number of reasons. Several editions of the T'ai Hsüan Ching are extant, of different dates and compilations. Although these editions (at least six of them) have different formats, type-faces, and editorial notes, the basic text is virtually the same. These 'standard' editions are all available in modern reprints, and access to them is usually readily available in the libraries of Universities which have large oriental departments. A list of the modern reprints is given in the bibliography.

Whatever the imprint of these 'standard' editions, they fall into one of two versions: one based on an edition by Ssu Ma Kuang 司馬光 AD 1019-1086, and the other, of a similar period, with commentaries by Fang Wang, an appendix by Wang Yai, and philological notes by Lin Yü. The only difference between these two versions of the text is the nature of the editorial glosses, described below. Whatever the date or imprint, all versions of the 'standard' texts have the following scheme:

1. The tetragram of four lines (e.g. 𝌣).
2. (Usually in lighter type) An analysis of the lines of the tetragram, after the nomenclature of Yang Hsiung. For example, the tetragram above would be analysed thus: 二方一州一部三家 That is to say,

Square 2, division 1, department 1, family 3.

3. The title, or name, of the Shou. (Always a single character.)
4. Some editorial explanation of the Shou title.
5. The opening, philosophical, verse.
6. An explanation of this opening philosophical statement.
7. The phrase Ch'u I (初 一), meaning First Chief, and supposed to be the first of the nine divisions of the text into Tsan, or subdivisions.
8. (Continuing from (7.) without a break) A line from Yang Hsiung's text.
9. A gloss on the above line of text.
10. The phrase Ts'e Yüeh (測 曰), meaning, 'the interpretation says . . .'
11. (Continuing from (10.) without a break) Text, in heavy print, as if original text, and not an editorial gloss (see below) similar in content to (8.) above.
12. An editorial gloss on (11.).
13. The phrase Tz'u Erh (次 二), second assistant, and supposed to be the second Tsan (see (7.) above).
14. A continuation of the text.
15. A gloss on the text just given . . .

and so on and so forth, each fragment of the original text generating its own glosses, interpretation, and glosses on the interpretations. The validity of all this encumbrance of text will be discussed in a moment. Firstly, let us look at the nature of the text as it appears in Ch'en Jen Hsi's edition. (In order to compare the Ch'en Jen Hsi version with the 'standard' versions described above, the same numeration is retained).

1. Nowhere in the Ch'en Jen Hsi edition do the tetragrams appear; neither in the texts of the Shou themselves, nor in the preface, nor table of contents, nor in the appendix.
2. Since there are no tetragrams, there are no analyses of the lines of the tetragrams.
3. In one or two cases the title characters of the Shou vary, but only in the sense that a stroke or two in a different place changes the meaning of the character. There is no major difference in the written character. Where such alternative readings occur, these are indicated in the notes to this present edition.
4. If the title of the Shou is in doubt, so must be the gloss on the title.
5. The opening 'philosophical statement' is often much shorter than that given in the standard editions, and may even be absent. This

is particularly the case with the latter Shou.

6. The glosses, where they appear, are quite different. Sometimes they intrude on the text, to explain an unusual character, or clarify a difficult expression. (For examples of these glosses of Ch'en Jen Hsi, see Shou 32).

7., 10., 13. The phrases Ch'u I, Ts'e Yüeh, and Tz'u Erh appear nowhere in the texts, neither in the Shou themselves, nor anywhere else. It follows, therefore, that all the glosses on these lines, and the interpretations, will not appear.

Obviously, we have to ask why it was that Ch'en Jen Hsi's edition did not include all these lines and interpretations which are found in all other editions. There are three possible answers: either (a) Ch'en Jen Hsi deliberately produced, and published, a much-watered down version of the classic text for reasons best known to himself; (b) that he was unaware of the existence of complete versions of the text (the 'standard' versions are based on reprints of Sung dynasty copies); or (c) he had access to a copy which he believed to be far older, and therefore much closer to Yang Hsiung's original, than any edition circulating in the Ming period.

In order to decide which of these alternatives is the most likely, it is important to remember that Ch'en Jen Hsi was not only one of the Imperial Examiners, and a compiler of the massive Imperial Encyclopaedia, but that he was also an expert on Chou dynasty official biography. If he had produced slip-shod work (as a careless, dashed-off edition of the T'ai Hsüan would have been seen to be) there would have been a remarkable opportunity for his enemies (there must have been many failed examinees with a grudge against him) to hold him up to ridicule. It follows therefore that the first two alternative possibilities do not bear consideration. On the other hand, the more one ponders the third possibility, the more intriguing it becomes.

The Ming dynasty was in a state of collapse; Ch'en Jen Hsi was busy compiling the Imperial Encyclopaedia; meanwhile in addition, he would have his other usual duties to perform. What could have been so momentous that it prompted him to lay all these worries to one side, and begin work on the edition of an ancient text which was already known to scholars? (Indeed, Ch'en Jen Hsi quotes no less than seven authorities who had praised the T'ai Hsüan Ching, among them Pan Ku, the historian who died in AD92, and the third century astronomer Lu Chi, who foretold his own death). The most likely solution, and one which neatly answers so many problems, is that Ch'en Jen Hsi, while browsing through the Imperial archives, stumbled across a manuscript which was such an exciting find that he at once cast aside all the pressing needs of the moment to put it before the public; a manuscript which he believed was the oldest extant copy of a work which those ancient authorities had regarded as even superior to the I Ching. If it were not Yang Hsiung's own manuscript, it must have been at least older than any version known to Ch'en Jen Hsi. He had the manuscript copied for publication, shorn of all the later Sung additions, only interpolating his own explanations of ancient or obscure characters and phrases. The copy in the British Library, published probably in 1632, is therefore likely to be much closer to Yang Hsiung's original text (if not actually based on Yang Hsiung's own manuscript) than are the reprints of Sung dynasty (AD960-1297) version.

The conclusion is that the 'standard' versions contain much extraneous material interpolated by a later hand — at the moment unknown. It seems likely that the earliest editors had perforce to supply their own 'Tsan' with subsequent interpretations, and follow these interpretations with further glosses of their own. (It is not uncommon for scholars to write their own footnotes). Once pruned of such apocryphal material, the remaining texts are often extremely short — for example, Shou 77 consists of only eleven characters; scarcely enough material to construct an opening verse, let alone a further nine Tsan, or sub-divisions. At the other extreme, some of the Shou are long enough to cover the nine Tsan and still have material left over. It is easy to understand the problems of those early scholars who wanted to turn to the T'ai Hsüan to answer their own particular problems. The text had to be unravelled, divided into Tsan, and further interpreted; the sybilline verses were abstruse enough in the first place, without the additional difficulty of knowing which verses (often arranged in contradictory pairs) pertained to the situation in question.

The same problems, of course, face the present writer. Every endeavour, however, has been made to leave the text unadorned, shorn of glosses, and anything else that would intrude on the text. Such explanatory notes have been gathered together separately. Regarding the division into Tsan, this has been done as discreetly as possible, bearing in mind that *these are the present writer's own interpretations*; no division into Tsan is given in the text of Ch'en Jen Hsi, which is, as we have seen, the version most likely to be that closest to Yang Hsiung's original text.

The complete text has never before been translated into any other language, although occasional passages from it have been. Possibly the earliest is the quotation in Giles' Dictionary from Shou 3 (see the commentary). Three lengthy passages, based on the 'standard' edition, were translated into Russian by Shchutskii, and these have been re-translated into English from the Russian. The advantage of this text is that it enables the reader to compare not only the style of translation, but the differences between the Ch'en Jen Hsi and 'standard' texts.

There are lengthy quotations from the essays and other writings by Yang Hsiung in Feng Yu Lan's *Chinese Philosophy*, but no significant passages from the Shou texts themselves.

No. 2 Chou
Rotation

HEAD:

The pneuma of Light rotates its spirit
And returns to the beginning.
The creatures follow [it] according to [their] type.

STROPHES:

1. You return to the heart of heaven.
Such pretense of [personal] powers!
Evil!

SOLUTION:

The evil of the return to the heart [of heaven],
This is intolerance of the core.

2. You erect the axis of the core.
In the rotation there are no angles.

SOLUTION:

Erect the axis of the core,
Establish the principal thought.

3. Issuing from yourself, retiring into yourself
[You] polar star of happiness and unhappiness.

SOLUTION:

In issuing from oneself and retiring into oneself,
It is impossible not to be watchful.

4. You gird yourself with a leather belt and buckle,
On it attach a jasper ring.

SOLUTION:

You gird yourself with a leather belt and buckle,
You restrain yourself, you bind.

5. In the centre of the earth is your hut,
Prepare your golden chariot.
But even this advice will pass.

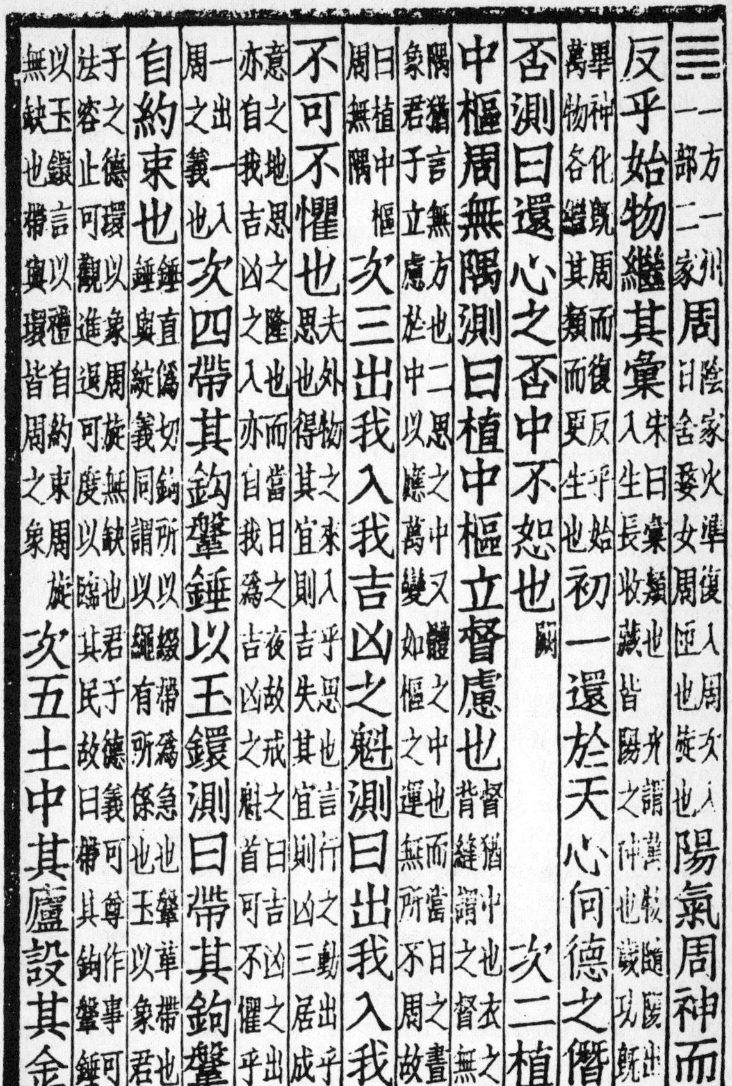
一方一州一部二家周陰家火準復入周次入日舍嬰女周匝也旋也陽氣周神而
反乎始物繼其彙宋曰彙類也光謂萬物隨陽出入生長收藏皆陽之神也歲功既
畢神化既周而復反乎始萬物各繼其類而更生也初一還於天心何德之僭
否測曰還心之否中不恕也[illegible]次二植
中樞周無隅測曰植中樞立督慮也督猶中也衣之背縫謂之督無
隅猶言無方也二思之中又體之中也而當日之晝象君子立慮於中以應萬變如樞之運無所不周故
日植中樞周無隅次三出我入我吉凶之魁測曰出我入我
不可不懼也夫外物之來入乎思也言行之動出乎思也得其宜則吉失其宜則凶三居成
意之地思之隆也而當日之夜故戒之曰吉凶之出亦自我吉凶之入亦自我爲吉凶之魁首可不懼乎
一出一入周之義也次四帶其鉤鞶鍾以玉鐶測曰帶其鉤鞶
自約束也鍾直偽切鉤所以綴帶爲急也鞶革帶也鍾與綻義同謂以繩有所係也玉以象君
子之德環以象周旋無缺也君子德義可尊作事可法容止可觀進退可度以臨其民故曰帶其鉤鞶鍾
以玉鐶言以禮自約束周旋無缺也帶與環皆周之象次五土中其廬設其金

The beginning of the text of Shou 2 in the 'standard' editions. Note the commentary lines, and the 'interpretations' of these additional remarks. The translation alongside is from the English translation of Shchutskii's 'Researches on the I Ching'.

In this version of the T'ai Hsüan Ching, attempts have been made to try and retain the 'laconic' quality of the original language, by translating, wherever possible, each phrase word by word, and keeping syntax words (including the verb 'to be') to a minimum. Ideally, the result would be an epigrammatic style that would embody the quintessential meaning, (as one finds in such expressions as 'the more the merrier' or 'finders keepers'). Unfortunately the result, more often than not, tends towards a telegraphic style reminiscent of newspaper headlines (such as 'General travels back to front'). But I feel that even this is preferable to a high-style of translation which might distort the 'feel' of the original. Indeed, the lack of gender, tense, and number gives the original a kind of ambiguous quality which is, dare one suggest, ideally suited to texts of a prognosticatory character. (At one point, in a fit of purist enthusiasm, I even toyed with the idea of translating the whole text in monosyllables; this task, I am very much afraid, defeated me in its earliest stages, but it is nevertheless an idea which I throw out for future translators).

There are certain words in the text which have to be explained; not so much the technical terms such as Shou, Tsan, and the like, which can be explained in a glossary, but basic ideas relating to Chinese philosophy or civilization. The use of the word 'knight' may seem to be an anachronism, but it does convey, in a single word, the idea of a 'gentleman and a scholar' or 'man of refinement'. (Actually, the Chinese expression uses two characters; literally translated as 'chief's son'). Yin and Yang are almost untranslatable, but Yang Ch'i (陽氣) has been translated as 'active flux' on the thirty-odd occasions when this term appears in the text.

The character Wu (物) has been translated as 'element' whenever it appears on its own, in which case it means 'the particular quality of that Shou'. However, when it follows the character Wan (萬), myriad, or ten thousand, it has the meaning 'every single thing in the universe'. Briefly, Chinese philosophy held that there was originally the Great Unity; this divided into Yin and Yang, and by a process of sub-division, the 'ten-thousand things' were formed. The word 'element' has clearly no connection with the four elements of Aristotle, the five elements of Chinese philosophy, nor the ninety-odd elements of modern chemistry.

The word 'abyss' appears frequently; this has both the meaning 'valley, ravine' as well as 'chaos, outer space'. Compare Shou 20 'advancing through the abyss, the knight uses a boat' where abyss is used in its material sense of ravine or valley, with Shou 81 'hoarded in the heart of the abyss' which refers to the Sun hidden in the darkness during Winter. Thus, in Shou 19, 'Yang skips in the abyss' can mean both lambs skipping in the valleys, and the active forces energizing remote space (recalling Genesis).

Whenever the word Tao (道) appears, meaning road, or path, it can be taken that this also means the 'true path' (the 'Tao' of Taoism). Another common character in the T'ai Hsüan Ching is Fang (方) meaning square, or direction. The difficulty here is that Fang is the technical term used to describe the topmost line of the tetragrams; also, according to Ch'en Jen Hsi, it was another expression for the Tao. A number of these secondary meanings are referred to in the commentaries to the Shou texts.

The woodblock-printed text published by Ch'en Jen Hsi was not always easy to read; sometimes the blocks had been over-inked, smudging the characters, while in other cases, under-inking resulted in ghostly, illegible print. Occasionally a character would be chipped; elsewhere, a stray chip added a supernumerary dot or stroke to a character, changing its meaning completely. For these reasons, occasional recourse was made to the 'standard' editions when the Ch'en Jen Hsi text was in doubt; though it must be added that the 'standard' versions themselves were not ever reliable, as is evident from the frequent inversion or mis-interpretation of the Shou tetragrams. Whenever doubt existed concerning a passage, this has been noted in the commentaries. (Of particular interest is the title of Shou 8, the interpretation of which considerably alters the meaning of the text itself).

The Calendar of the T'ai Hsüan

There is no immediately apparent correlation between the number of Shou 81 and the number of days in the year; this makes it all the more remarkable that Yang Hsiung could have proposed a calendar system based on the T'ai Hsüan. It has been suggested by at least one scholar (W. Eberhard) that the original purpose of the T'ai Hsüan was in fact a calendrical system based on the then new guide-lines laid down by the astronomers Liu Hsin and Liu Hsiang during the first century BC, either a few years before, or at the same time, that Yang Hsiung was writing the text of the T'ai Hsüan. But in view of the great interest which the I Ching held for Yang Hsiung, it seems to me that he hit upon his calendrical system only after he had studied the philosophical manifestations of the 81 Shou.

The Chinese calendar, even as it stands today, is far from being uncomplicated; there are twelve, or occasionally thirteen, months in the year, which is in turn divided into twenty-four fortnights. In addition to the mean solar year of, on average, 365 days, runs another 'cyclical' year of 360 days, divided into 36 weeks of ten days each. Add to this the fact that the Chinese, at least in our present era, also have to contend with a working week of 7 days.

Yang Hsiung divided the year into 81 Shou of 4½ days each. At first sight this may seem an eccentric choice, but if instead of the 81 Shou, we consider the sub-divisions into 729 Tsan, we arrive at a figure which is related to the length of the mean solar year, in that the 'middle' number in the series 1 to 729 is actually 365 (see the section on Magic Squares, page 46). In other words, according to Yang Hsiung's calendar, the year could be divided into 729 Tsan, each being half a day, forenoon or afternoon, with only one of the Tsan being a whole day to ensure that the year ended at midnight.

The 729 Tsan, forming the 81 Shou, were gathered into nine *T'ien* (天) 'seasons' or 'heavens'. The names of these principal divisions were taken from the first Shou in each *T'ien*. A glance at the names of these principal Shou will indicate that they are related. For example, the names of the 55th, 64th, and 73rd Shou are Diminishing, Chien (減), Sinking, Chen (沉), and Completing, Ch'eng (成); these being the 7th, 8th, and 9th *T'ien* respectively.

Yang Hsiung indicated that the year began in the eleventh month, finishing in the tenth (of what is the present Chinese calendar). This would seem to suggest that Yang Hsiung's calendar began with the New Moon which preceeded the Winter Solstice, since the Chinese calendar was so constructed (by the use of inter-calary months) that the eleventh month always included the Winter Solstice.

All Chinese months begin with the New Moon, as observed at Peking. Fortunately, this makes it very easy to make a correspondence between Yang Hsiung's calendar and the present Western one. In fact, it is much easier than it would have been had Yang Hsiung tried to apply his *T'ien*, Shou and Tsan to the Chinese calendar as it stood, since the average difference in the number of days between January 1 and Yang Hsiung's New Year's Day is much less than the average difference between January 1 and the present Chinese New Year, which can fall as late as February 20 (as it does in 1985).

In this way, the nine *T'ien* accord perfectly well with the progress of the seasons of the year. For example, if Yang Hsiung's calendar is taken as commencing a week or so before the Winter Solstice the third *T'ien*, Ts'ung, would correspond to the period from about the middle of March to the end of April. The character Ts'ung (從) means 'compliance, obedience' in general usage, but also means 'to plough in a North to South direction'. Furthermore, the text for Ts'ung begins: '*Yang skips in the valleys, in the fields, in the marshes, on the mountain tops*' which is not only a direct reference to the beginning of Spring, but could also be a pun on the word Yang. In the text Yang is written 陽 meaning 'male, positive'. But Yang written 羊 means 'sheep' which do, of course, skip and gambol in the Spring. As a further point here, it might be that there is a pun on Yang Hsiung's own name as well.

Unfortunately, this system, as elegant as it might appear to be, does pose one problem. Since the Chinese year has a variable number of days (from 355 when there is no intercalary month, to a possible 390) it is not possible to say that the calendar of Yang Hsiung begins *each year* with the first new moon before the Winter Solstice; otherwise there would be some years in which days were doubled — in other years, days would be left over without a calendar designation.

The calendar *has* to begin on a fixed date, and because it is of course possible for the New Moon to fall on the same day as the Winter Solstice (which statistically it will to do at least once every 31 years, but in practice does much more frequently, owing to calendar adjustments) it would seem reasonable to begin the fixed year with the Winter Solstice.

But for more specific, rather than general, correspondence, the text of Shou 41 (q.v.) is particularly revealing. This is the central Shou in the 9×9 grid of the 81 diagrams, and as such corresponds to the mid-point of the calendar. If the calendar began with the Winter Solstice, then this Shou would correspond to the Summer Solstice. There can be no doubt about the meaning of this text:

元 離 之 極

'The Chief brightness reaches its limits'.

Similar confirmation can be found in the texts which correspond to the equinoxes; from Shou 20, which would represent the Spring Equinox:

中 行 日 飛 懸 陰

'The central path of the Sun, flies suspended over the darkness of Yin' which seems to suggest a balance between the natures of darkness and light.

Having established that the calendar does in fact begin and end with the Winter Solstice, it is possible to equate each of the texts with definite dates in the solar year. That done, an even more remarkable observation can be made. The texts to Shou 67 and 68 are sufficiently abstruse for commentators to have regarded them as moral tenets. The title of Shou 67, Hui 悔 means *obscure* and the text begins:

日 正 中 月 正 隆

'The Sun is principal and central; the Moon is principal and surpassing'. What can be made of this? Later we read in the same Shou text:

睄 提 明 或 遷 之 行

'The Sun's brightness is reluctantly sent on a journey'. Now the word Hui, while it means *obscure*, also means *eclipse*. Read in this context, both lines make sense: it is a reference to an eclipse of the sun. Similarly, in the following Shou 68:

瞢 腹 睒 天 視 其 畛

'Dimness; division; then getting brighter. Heaven does not inspect its boundaries' can be interpreted as the passing of the eclipse.

These two Shou would correspond to the period October 14-19 and 20-24.

Le P. Pierre Hoang's '*Catalogue des eclipses de soleil et de lune relatées dans les documents chinois*' lists nineteen eclipses of the sun which occurred between 53BC and AD18 and which were recorded at Ch'ang An. Although these dates do not always tally with those in v. Oppolzer's '*Canon der Finsternisse*' (in fact one of the recorded eclipses is not even listed in v. Oppolzer) the charts appended to v. Oppolzer's Canon show that for the period in question four of the eclipses were total in the region of Ch'ang An. This is an important point because it must be remembered that eclipses in general are not infrequent, but rarely noted by the casual observer since there is no discernable perturbation of the daylight — no more than would be made by a small cloud — and certainly nothing of such remarkable occurrence that it would cause one to stare up at the sun shining at a latitude corresponding to that of the southern Mediterranean. Only total eclipses, with all their attendant phenomena, are sufficiently awe-inspiring. The paths of three of these total eclipses passed very close to Ch'ang An, where Yang Hsiung lived from AD13. These were the eclipses of 27BC (July 17) which also passed near the Cheng Tu region, where Yang Hsiung spent his earlier years; that of AD2 (November 23) and an annular eclipse in AD 6 (October 11). The latter, with its spectacular corona, would have been a magnificent sight, although this aspect of the eclipse would only be observable about a hundred miles north of Ch'ang An. The other eclipse, that of 25BC, is however of more particular interest. Like the eclipse of two years before, it would have been total or near-total in the Cheng Tu region, but unlike the other three eclipses, it would not have appeared exceptionally noteworthy in the capital. The date of this eclipse was October 23, so corresponding to Shou 68 of the T'ai Hsüan Ching. Perhaps it is not too far-fetched to suggest that Shou 68 is in fact a record of this eclipse, since it would certainly have been seen by the philosopher, in view of its near or complete totality.

While this does not mean, as a consequence, that the T'ai Hsüan Ching must have been written in that year or shortly afterwards, it does seem to imply that the work was written before AD2, because in that year Yang

Hsiung would have observed the total eclipse in Ch'ang An, and that eclipse, being fresher in his mind, would have been the one he recorded.

The text corresponding to November 23 is Shou 75; but neither this, nor the texts of the Shou 74 and 76, can be construed as referring to an eclipse.

The conclusions which might be drawn from this are therefore:

(a) the calendar of the T'ai Hsüan Ching begins with the Winter solstice;
(b) the texts of Shou 67 and 68, corresponding to the third week in October, refer to an eclipse of the Sun;
(c) it is likely that the eclipse was the one observable at Cheng Tu on October 23 25BC;
(d) the T'ai Hsüan Ching was written after 25 BC, and completed before AD 2, when Yang Hsiung would have had the opportunity to observe another total eclipse.

關子明擬元洞極經圖

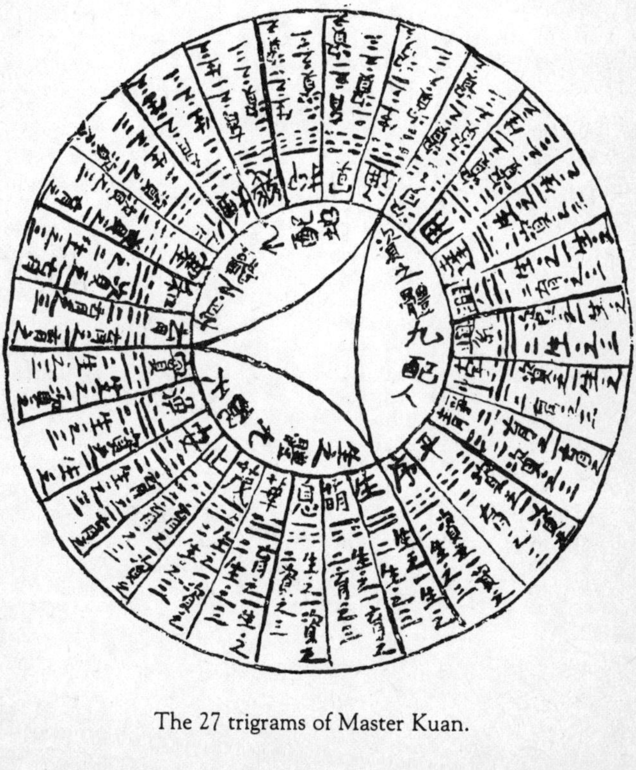

The 27 trigrams of Master Kuan.

THE CALENDAR OF THE T'AI HSÜAN

ORDINARY YEARS

	AM	PM		AM	PM		AM	PM		AM	PM
Dec 22	1	2	Feb 5	91	92	Mar 23	183	184	May 8	275	276
23	3	4	6	93	94	24	185	186	9	277	278
24	5	6	7	95	96	25	187	188	10	279	280
25	7	8	8	97	98	26	189	190	11	281	282
26	9	10	9	99	100	27	191	192	12	283	284
27	11	12	10	101	102	28	193	194	13	285	186
28	13	14	11	103	104	29	195	196	14	287	288
29	15	16	12	105	106	30	197	198	15	289	290
30	17	18	13	107	108	31	199	200	16	291	292
31	19	20	14	109	110	Apr 1	201	202	17	293	294
			15	111	112	2	203	204	18	295	296
JAN 1	21	22	16	113	114	3	205	206	19	297	298
2	23	24	17	115	116	4	207	208	20	299	300
3	25	26	18	117	118	5	209	210	21	301	302
4	27	28	19	119	120	6	211	212	22	303	304
5	29	30	20	121	122	7	213	214	23	305	306
6	31	32	21	123	124	8	215	216	24	307	308
7	33	34	22	125	126	9	217	218	25	309	310
8	35	36	23	127	128	10	219	220	26	311	312
9	37	38	24	129	130	11	221	222	27	313	314
10	39	40	25	131	132	12	223	224	28	315	316
11	41	42	26	133	134	13	225	226	29	317	318
12	43	44	27	135	136	14	227	228	30	319	320
13	45	46	28	137	138	15	229	230	31	321	322
14	47	48	Mar 1	139	140	16	231	232	Jun 1	323	324
15	49	50	2	141	142	17	233	234	2	325	326
16	51	52	3	143	144	18	235	236	3	327	328
17	53	54	4	145	146	19	237	238	4	329	330
18	55	56	5	147	148	20	239	240	5	331	332
19	57	58	6	149	150	21	241	242	6	333	334
20	59	60	7	151	152	22	243	244	7	335	336
21	61	62	8	153	154	23	245	246	8	337	338
22	63	64	9	155	156	24	247	248	9	339	340
23	65	66	10	157	158	25	249	250	10	341	342
24	67	68	11	159	160	26	251	252	11	343	344
25	69	70	12	161	162	27	253	254	12	345	346
26	71	72	13	163	164	28	255	256	13	347	348
27	73	74	14	165	166	29	257	258	14	349	350
28	75	76	15	167	168	30	259	260	15	351	352
29	77	78	16	169	170	May 1	261	262	16	353	354
30	79	80	17	171	172	2	263	264	17	355	356
31	81	82	18	173	174	3	265	266	18	357	358
Feb 1	83	84	19	175	176	4	267	268	19	359	360
2	85	86	20	177	178	5	269	270	20	361	362
3	87	88	21	179	180	6	271	272	21	363	364
4	89	90	22	181	182	7	273	274	22	365	365

ORDINARY YEARS cont.

	AM	PM		AM	PM		AM	PM		AM	PM
Jun 23	366	367	Aug 8	458	459	Sep 23	550	551	Nov 8	642	643
24	368	369	9	460	461	24	552	553	9	644	645
25	370	371	10	462	463	25	554	555	10	646	647
26	372	373	11	464	465	26	556	557	11	648	649
27	374	375	12	466	467	27	558	559	12	650	651
28	376	377	13	468	469	28	560	561	13	652	653
29	378	379	14	470	471	29	562	563	14	654	655
30	380	381	15	472	473	30	564	565	15	656	657
Jul 1	382	383	16	474	475	Oct 1	566	567	16	658	659
2	384	385	17	476	477	2	568	569	17	660	661
3	386	387	18	478	479	3	570	571	18	662	663
4	388	389	19	480	481	4	572	573	19	664	665
5	390	391	20	482	483	5	574	575	20	666	667
6	392	393	21	484	485	6	576	577	21	668	669
7	394	395	22	486	487	7	578	579	22	670	671
8	396	397	23	488	489	8	580	581	23	672	673
9	398	399	24	490	491	9	582	583	24	674	675
10	400	401	25	492	493	10	584	585	25	676	677
11	402	403	26	494	495	11	586	587	26	678	679
12	404	405	27	496	497	12	588	589	27	680	681
13	406	407	28	498	499	13	590	591	28	682	683
14	408	409	29	500	501	14	592	593	29	684	685
15	410	411	20	502	503	15	594	595	30	686	687
16	412	413	31	504	505	16	596	597	Dec 1	688	689
17	414	415	Sep 1	506	507	17	598	599	2	690	691
18	416	417	2	508	509	18	600	601	3	692	693
19	418	419	3	510	511	19	602	603	4	694	695
20	420	421	4	512	513	20	604	605	5	696	697
21	422	423	5	514	515	21	606	607	6	698	699
22	424	425	6	516	617	22	608	609	7	700	701
23	426	427	7	518	519	23	610	611	8	702	703
24	428	429	8	520	521	24	612	613	9	704	705
25	430	431	9	522	523	25	614	615	10	706	707
26	432	433	10	524	525	26	616	617	11	708	709
27	434	435	11	526	527	27	618	619	12	710	711
28	436	437	12	528	529	28	620	621	13	712	713
29	438	439	13	530	531	29	622	623	14	714	715
30	440	441	14	532	533	30	624	625	15	716	717
31	442	443	15	534	535	31	626	627	16	718	719
Aug 1	444	445	16	536	537	Nov 1	628	629	17	720	721
2	446	447	17	538	539	2	630	631	18	722	723
3	448	449	18	540	541	3	632	633	19	724	725
4	450	451	19	542	543	4	634	635	20	726	727
5	452	453	20	544	545	5	636	637	21	728	729
6	454	455	21	546	547	6	638	639			
7	456	457	22	548	549	7	640	641			

THE CALENDAR OF THE T'AI HSÜAN

LEAP YEARS

	AM	PM		AM	PM		AM	PM		AM	PM
Dec 22	1	1	Feb 5	90	91	Mar 22	182	183	May 7	274	275
23	2	3	6	92	93	23	184	185	8	276	277
24	4	5	7	94	95	24	186	187	9	278	279
25	6	7	8	96	97	25	188	189	10	280	281
26	8	9	9	98	99	26	190	191	11	282	283
27	10	11	10	100	101	27	192	193	12	284	285
28	12	13	11	102	103	28	194	195	13	286	287
29	14	15	12	104	105	29	196	197	14	288	289
30	16	17	13	106	107	30	198	199	15	290	291
31	18	19	14	108	109	31	200	201	16	292	293
			15	110	111	Apr 1	202	203	17	294	295
JAN 1	20	21	16	112	113	2	204	205	18	296	297
2	22	23	17	114	115	3	206	207	19	298	299
3	24	25	18	116	117	4	208	209	20	300	301
4	26	27	19	118	119	5	210	211	21	302	303
5	28	29	20	120	121	6	212	213	22	304	305
6	30	31	21	122	123	7	214	215	23	306	307
7	32	33	22	124	125	8	216	217	24	308	309
8	34	35	23	126	127	9	218	219	25	310	311
9	36	37	24	128	129	10	220	221	26	312	313
10	38	39	25	130	131	11	222	223	27	314	315
11	40	41	26	132	133	12	224	225	28	316	317
12	42	43	27	134	135	13	226	227	29	318	319
13	44	45	28	136	137	14	228	229	30	320	321
14	46	47	29	138	139	15	230	231	31	322	323
15	48	49	Mar 1	140	141	16	232	233	Jun 1	324	325
16	50	51	2	142	143	17	234	235	2	326	327
17	52	53	3	144	145	18	236	237	3	328	329
18	54	55	4	146	147	19	238	239	4	330	331
19	56	57	5	148	149	20	240	241	5	332	333
20	58	59	6	150	151	21	242	243	6	334	335
21	60	61	7	152	153	22	244	245	7	336	337
22	62	63	8	154	155	23	246	247	8	338	339
23	64	65	9	156	157	24	248	249	9	340	341
24	66	67	10	158	159	25	250	251	10	342	343
25	68	69	11	160	161	26	252	253	11	344	345
26	70	71	12	162	163	27	254	255	12	346	347
27	72	73	13	164	165	28	256	257	13	348	349
28	74	75	14	166	167	29	258	259	14	350	351
29	76	77	15	168	169	30	260	261	15	352	353
30	78	79	16	170	171	May 1	262	263	16	354	355
31	80	81	17	172	173	2	264	265	17	356	357
Feb 1	82	83	18	174	175	3	266	267	18	358	359
2	84	85	19	176	177	4	268	269	19	360	361
3	86	87	20	178	179	5	270	271	20	362	363
4	88	89	21	180	181	6	272	273	21	364	365

LEAP YEARS cont.

	AM	PM		AM	PM		AM	PM		AM	PM
Jun 22	365	366	Aug 7	457	458	Sep 22	549	550	Nov 7	641	642
23	367	368	8	459	460	23	551	552	8	643	644
24	369	370	9	461	462	24	553	554	9	645	646
25	371	372	10	463	464	25	555	556	10	647	648
26	373	374	11	465	466	26	557	558	11	649	650
27	375	376	12	467	468	27	559	560	12	651	652
28	377	378	13	469	470	28	561	562	13	653	654
29	379	380	14	471	472	29	563	564	14	655	656
30	381	382	15	473	474	30	565	566	15	657	658
Jul 1	383	384	16	475	476	Oct 1	567	568	16	659	660
2	385	386	17	477	478	2	569	570	17	661	662
3	387	388	18	479	480	3	571	572	18	663	664
4	389	390	19	481	482	4	573	574	19	665	666
5	391	392	20	483	484	5	575	576	20	667	668
6	393	394	21	485	486	6	577	578	21	669	670
7	395	396	22	487	488	7	579	580	22	671	672
8	397	398	23	489	490	8	581	582	23	673	674
9	399	400	24	491	492	9	583	584	24	675	676
10	401	402	25	493	494	10	585	586	25	677	678
11	403	404	26	495	496	11	587	588	26	679	680
12	405	406	27	497	498	12	589	590	27	681	682
13	407	408	28	499	500	13	591	592	28	683	684
14	409	410	29	501	502	14	593	594	29	685	686
15	411	412	30	503	504	15	595	596	30	687	688
16	413	414	31	505	506	16	597	598	Dec 1	689	690
17	415	416	Sep 1	507	508	17	599	600	2	691	692
18	417	418	2	509	510	18	601	602	3	693	694
19	419	420	3	511	512	19	603	604	4	695	696
20	421	422	4	513	514	20	605	606	5	697	698
21	423	424	5	515	516	21	607	608	6	699	700
22	425	426	6	517	518	22	609	610	7	701	702
23	427	428	7	519	520	23	611	612	8	703	704
24	429	430	8	521	522	24	613	614	9	705	706
25	431	432	9	523	524	25	615	616	10	707	708
26	433	434	10	525	526	26	617	618	11	709	710
27	435	436	11	527	528	27	619	620	12	711	712
28	437	438	12	529	530	28	621	622	13	713	714
29	439	440	13	531	532	29	623	624	14	715	716
30	441	442	14	533	534	30	625	626	15	717	718
31	443	444	15	535	536	31	627	628	16	719	720
Aug 1	445	446	16	537	538	Nov 1	629	630	17	721	722
2	447	448	17	539	540	2	631	632	18	723	724
3	449	450	18	541	542	3	633	634	19	725	726
4	451	452	19	543	544	4	635	636	20	727	728
5	453	454	20	545	546	5	637	638	21	729	729
6	455	456	21	547	548	6	639	640			

TO FIND THE *T'IEN* AND SHOU

Tsan	Shou	*T'ien*	Tsan	Shou	*T'ien*
1- 9	1	1	365-369	41	5
10- 18	2	1	370-378	42	5
19- 27	3	1	379-387	43	5
28- 36	4	1	388-396	44	5
37- 45	5	1	397-405	45	5
46- 54	6	1	406-414	46	6
55- 63	7	1	415-423	47	6
64- 72	8	1	424-432	48	6
73- 81	9	1	433-441	49	6
82- 90	10	2	442-450	50	6
91- 99	11	2	451-459	51	6
100-108	12	2	460-468	52	6
109-117	13	2	469-477	53	6
118-126	14	2	478-486	54	6
127-135	15	2	487-495	55	7
136-144	16	2	496-504	56	7
145-153	17	2	505-513	57	7
154-162	18	2	514-522	58	7
163-171	19	3	523-531	59	7
172-180	20	3	532-540	60	7
181-189	21	3	541-549	61	7
190-198	22	3	550-558	62	7
199-207	23	3	559-567	63	7
208-216	24	3	568-576	64	8
209-225	25	3	577-585	65	8
226-234	26	3	586-594	66	8
235-243	27	3	595-603	67	8
244-252	28	4	604-612	68	8
253-261	29	4	613-621	69	8
262-270	30	4	622-630	70	8
271-279	31	4	631-639	71	8
280-288	32	4	640-648	72	8
289-297	33	4	649-657	73	9
298-306	34	4	658-666	74	9
307-315	35	4	667-675	75	9
316-324	36	4	676-684	76	9
325-333	37	5	685-693	77	9
334-342	38	5	694-702	78	9
343-351	39	5	703-711	79	9
352-360	40	5	712-720	80	9
361-365	41	5	721-729	81	9

CONSULTING THE T'AI HSÜAN CHING

There are three basic methods which can be used to consult the T'ai Hsüan Ching: the horoscopic, numerological, and milfoil.

Additionally, some other systems based on combinations of these three methods could well be employed.

The horoscopic method is self-evident: an important date (the birth-date, the day that the question is being posed, or the date of the event in question) is chosen. The Calendar of the T'ai Hsüan is then consulted to search out the relevant Tsan, following which reference is made to the appropriate Shou.

In numerological methods, three co-ordinates are taken; these could be, for example, the questioner's name, his birthplace, and his date of birth. The number of letters in the words are added together and divided by 9, and the remainder noted (a remainder of 0 is regarded as 9); or else the digits are added together, and similarly divided by 9 to extract the remainder. These three remainders give three co-ordinates, of which the first will refer the questioner to the *T'ien*, the second to the Shou in that *T'ien*, and the third to the Tsan within the Shou.

The third system, using milfoil stalks (as in the I Ching) or bamboo slips, is dealt with at length later.

A more elaborate numerological method (which can also be combined with the horoscopic method) is to use the 'Magic Squares of 729 Tsan'. In these arrangements of nine magic squares (that is, an arrangement of numbers in which each row, vertically and horizontally, adds up to the same figure) all the numbers of the Tsan, from 1 to 729, have been arranged in such an intricate manner that not only is each of the nine squares a 'magic' arrangement, but if they are to be imagined laid one upon the other, in a stack of nine layers, every row and column throughout the cube so formed will also add up to the same total (3285). What is further remarkable is that at the very centre of the central magic square (from whatever direction the stack is looked at) is 365, the number of days in the year.

This central figure of 365 is the clue to the whole concept of the T'ai Hsüan Ching, for it not only explains the relationship between the Magic Squares and the calendar, but the harmony of numbers between the calendar and the Shou: there is more than one reason why the very first Shou is not called 'beginning', 'principal' or something as predictable, but 'Centre'. The whole calendar, the Magic Squares, and the T'ai Hsüan itself *revolves* (as the text frequently tells us) round the Centre — 365, or the number of days in the year. No wonder that many ancient sages perceived the T'ai Hsüan Ching to be a work of such mathematical elegance and numerological harmony. The division of four lines into three pieces was not an arbitrary piece of invention, but a skilful, and carefully thought-out means of encompassing the 729 Tsan according to the ways of the I Ching.

From the Magic Squares, it is possible to construct yet another way of consulting the T'ai Hsüan Ching. Once the three co-ordinates are obtained, the Tsan is found among the Magic Squares by the intersection of the Faces, Layers, and Slices. These terms describe the three directions from which one may look at a cube — the Face being front to back, the Layer top to bottom, and the Slice from side to side. Using one co-ordinate to find the Face, the second co-ordinate to find the Layer, and the third to get to the relevant Slice, one will then arrive at a figure where these three squares all meet.

This might be hard to visualize, but it is the same as first deciding on which *row* of the Magic Squares contains the Tsan (numbering the bottom row of each Magic Square, given in these pages, as 1), then choosing *which* Magic Square from the second co-ordinate, and the *column* in that Magic Square to find the final figure. (The Magic Squares can be found in their entirety in the Appendix on pages 201ff.)

The Lo Shu

I imagine that most readers will already be familiar with the Lo Shu, the River Diagram, or Magic Square of Nine Numbers. Known to Confucius, who bemoans in the Lun Yü (*Analects*)* 'The river gives forth no more diagrams', it is probably the earliest known representation of a magic square. The nine digits were each considered to have their own lucky or unlucky significance; equated with the nine half-tetragrams. Their meanings were as follows:

1	Chi	吉	Good luck
2	Chiu	咎	Error
3	Hsiang	祥	A portent (lucky or unlucky; generally taken to mean good fortune, unless qualified)
4	Lin	文	Regrets, repentance
5	P'ing	平	Even; unremarkable
6	Hui	悔	Regrets, rejection (Cf. Shou 67)
7	Tsai	災	Catastrophe (Fire and Water) Natural disasters.
8	Hsiu	休	Fortune: generally good, unless qualified, when it means the ups and downs of fortune
9	Hsiung	凶	Evil; bad luck

*Book 9, Chap. 8.

The Diagram of the Magic Square of Nine Numbers. Here, the Nine Integers are arranged in the form of the 3×3 Mathematical Magic Square, Lo Shu.

Error 咎 Chiu	Evil 凶 Hsiung	Regret 文 Lin
Calamity 災 Tsai	Average 平 P'ing	Portent 祥 Hsiang
Rejection 悔 Hui	Lucky 吉 Chi	Fortune 休 Hsiu

The Lo Shu Magic Square
(corresponding with the above)

2	9	4
7	5	3
6	1	8

A tortoise magic square printed from slips of wood and used in Tibet as a protection against evil spirits.

The Tetragrams Seen as Pairs of Bigrams

Mutationists (those who study the I Ching) often pay great attention to the structure of the lines of the diagrams. In the same way, each of the 81 Shou could be regarded as being formed from a pair of bigrams; the upper two lines being the Fang and Chou of the tetragram, the lower two the Pu and the Chia.

For example, tetragram 11 could be regarded as a doubling of bigram 2.

Similarly, tetragram 31 is the fourth bigram repeated, .

While tetragram 13, shows bigram 2 in the upper half and bigram 4 in the lower half.

Each of the nine bigrams form at least one tetragram by doubling itself; in some cases (when the lines are dissimilar) it is possible to form another bigram by reversal, or reflection. The auspices of the tetragrams can therefore be interpreted in the light of the component bigrams, and the prevalence, or otherwise, of good and bad omens.

Bigram	The Doubled bigram	The Reflected bigram	Reversals of the bigrams
1	1		41 81
2	11	29	31
3	21	57	71
4	31	13	11
5	41		1 81
6	51	69	71
7	61	25	21
8	71	53	51
9	81		1 41

Illustration of the Doubles and Reflections of the Bigrams.

The combinations of bigrams which form the 81 Shou can be read off the following table, also known as the '9×9 Magic Square of Integers'. (The use of the expression 'Magic Square' has in this case nothing to do with magic squares in the mathematical sense of the word.)

Lower bigram (Pu + Chia)	Upper bigram (Fang + Chou) 1	2	3	4	5	6	7	8	9
1	1	10	19	28	37	46	55	64	73
2	2	11	20	29	38	47	56	65	74
3	3	12	21	30	39	48	57	66	75
4	4	13	22	31	40	49	58	67	76
5	5	14	23	32	41	50	59	68	77
6	6	15	24	33	42	51	60	69	78
7	7	16	25	34	43	52	61	70	79
8	8	17	26	35	44	53	62	71	80
9	9	18	27	36	45	54	63	72	81

THE TSAN ASPECTS
RELATIVE TO THE MAGIC SQUARE OF NINE NUMBERS (1)

1	1	42	1	83	7	124	7	165	4	206	4	247	1	288	1	329	7
2	5	43	5	84	2	125	2	166	8	207	8	248	5	289	9	330	2
3	9	44	9	85	6	126	6	167	3	208	7	249	9	290	4	331	6
4	4	45	4	86	1	127	5	168	7	209	2	250	4	291	8	332	1
5	8	46	3	87	5	128	9	169	2	210	6	251	8	292	3	333	5
6	3	47	7	88	9	129	4	170	6	211	1	252	3	293	7	334	4
7	7	48	2	89	4	130	8	171	1	212	5	253	2	294	2	335	8
8	2	49	6	90	8	131	3	172	9	213	9	254	6	295	6	336	3
9	6	50	1	91	7	132	7	173	4	214	4	255	1	296	1	337	7
10	5	51	5	92	2	133	2	174	8	215	8	256	5	297	5	338	2
11	9	52	9	93	6	134	6	175	3	216	3	257	9	298	4	339	6
12	4	53	4	94	1	135	1	176	7	217	2	258	4	299	8	340	1
13	8	54	8	95	5	136	9	177	2	218	6	259	8	300	3	341	5
14	3	55	7	96	9	137	4	178	6	219	1	260	3	301	7	342	9
15	7	56	2	97	4	138	8	179	1	220	5	261	7	302	2	343	8
16	2	57	6	98	8	139	3	180	5	221	9	262	6	303	6	344	3
17	6	58	1	99	3	140	7	181	4	222	4	263	1	304	1	345	7
18	1	59	5	100	2	141	2	182	8	223	8	264	5	305	5	346	2
19	9	60	9	101	6	142	6	183	3	224	3	265	9	306	9	347	6
20	4	61	4	102	1	143	1	184	7	225	7	266	4	307	8	348	1
21	8	62	8	103	5	144	5	185	2	226	6	267	8	308	3	349	5
22	3	63	3	104	9	145	4	186	6	227	1	268	3	309	7	350	9
23	7	64	2	105	4	146	8	187	1	228	5	269	7	310	2	351	4
24	2	65	6	106	8	147	3	188	5	229	9	270	2	311	6	352	3
25	6	66	1	107	3	148	7	189	9	230	4	271	1	312	1	353	7
26	1	67	5	108	7	149	2	190	8	231	8	272	5	313	5	354	2
27	5	68	9	109	6	150	6	191	3	232	3	273	9	314	9	355	6
28	4	69	4	110	1	151	1	192	7	233	7	274	4	315	4	356	1
29	8	70	8	111	5	152	5	193	2	234	2	275	8	316	3	357	5
30	3	71	3	112	9	153	9	194	6	235	1	276	3	317	7	358	9
31	7	72	7	113	4	154	8	195	1	236	5	277	7	318	2	359	4
32	2	73	6	114	8	155	3	196	5	237	9	278	2	319	6	360	8
33	6	74	1	115	3	156	7	197	9	238	4	279	6	320	1	361	7
34	1	75	5	116	7	157	2	198	4	239	8	280	5	321	5	362	2
35	5	76	9	117	2	158	6	199	3	240	3	281	9	322	9	363	6
36	9	77	4	118	1	159	1	200	7	241	7	282	4	323	4	364	1
37	8	78	8	119	5	160	5	201	2	242	2	283	8	324	8	365	5
38	3	79	3	120	9	161	9	202	6	243	6	284	3	325	9	366	9
39	7	80	7	121	4	162	4	203	1	244	7	285	7	326	4	367	4
40	2	81	2	122	8	163	5	204	5	245	2	286	2	327	8	368	8
41	6	82	3	123	3	164	9	205	9	246	6	287	6	328	3	369	3

THE TSAN ASPECTS
RELATIVE TO THE MAGIC SQUARE OF NINE NUMBERS (2)

370	2	410	9	450	5	490	7	530	3	570	5	610	1	650	3	690	8
371	6	411	4	451	4	491	2	531	7	571	9	611	5	651	7	691	3
372	1	412	8	452	8	492	6	532	6	572	4	612	9	652	2	692	7
373	5	413	3	453	3	493	1	533	1	573	8	613	8	653	6	693	2
374	9	414	7	454	7	494	5	534	5	574	3	614	3	654	1	694	1
375	4	415	6	455	2	495	9	535	9	575	7	615	7	655	5	695	5
376	8	416	1	456	6	496	8	536	4	576	2	616	2	656	9	696	9
377	3	417	5	457	1	497	3	537	8	577	1	617	6	657	4	697	4
378	7	418	9	458	5	498	7	538	3	578	5	618	1	658	3	698	8
379	6	419	4	459	9	499	2	539	7	579	9	619	5	659	7	699	3
380	1	420	8	460	8	500	6	540	2	580	4	620	9	660	2	700	7
381	5	421	3	461	3	501	1	541	1	581	8	621	4	661	6	701	2
382	9	422	7	462	7	502	5	542	5	582	3	622	3	662	1	702	6
383	4	423	2	463	2	503	9	543	9	583	7	623	7	663	5	703	5
384	8	424	1	464	6	504	4	544	4	584	2	624	2	664	9	704	9
385	3	425	5	465	1	505	3	545	8	585	6	625	6	665	4	705	4
386	7	426	9	466	5	506	7	546	3	586	5	626	1	666	8	706	8
387	2	427	4	467	9	507	2	547	7	587	9	627	5	667	7	707	3
388	1	428	8	468	4	508	6	548	2	588	4	628	9	668	2	708	7
389	5	429	3	469	3	509	1	549	6	589	8	629	4	669	6	709	2
390	9	430	7	470	7	510	5	550	5	590	3	630	8	670	1	710	6
391	4	431	2	471	2	511	9	551	9	591	7	631	7	671	5	711	1
392	8	432	6	472	6	512	4	552	4	592	2	632	2	672	9	712	9
393	3	433	5	473	1	513	8	553	8	593	6	633	6	673	4	713	4
394	7	434	9	474	5	514	7	554	3	594	1	634	1	674	8	714	8
395	2	435	4	475	9	515	2	555	7	595	9	635	5	675	3	715	3
396	6	436	8	476	4	516	6	556	2	596	4	636	9	676	2	716	7
397	5	437	3	477	8	517	1	557	6	597	8	637	4	677	6	717	2
398	9	438	7	478	7	518	5	558	1	598	3	638	8	678	1	718	6
399	4	439	2	479	2	519	9	559	9	599	7	639	3	679	5	719	1
400	8	440	6	480	6	520	4	560	4	600	2	640	2	680	9	720	5
401	7	441	1	481	1	521	8	561	8	601	6	641	6	681	4	721	4
402	7	442	9	482	5	522	3	562	3	602	1	642	1	682	8	722	8
403	2	443	4	483	9	523	2	563	7	603	5	643	5	683	3	723	3
404	6	444	8	484	4	524	6	564	2	604	4	644	9	684	7	724	7
405	1	445	3	485	8	525	1	565	6	605	8	645	4	685	6	725	2
406	2	446	7	486	3	526	5	566	1	606	3	646	8	686	1	726	6
407	6	447	2	487	4	527	9	567	5	607	7	647	3	687	5	727	1
408	1	448	6	488	8	528	4	568	6	608	2	648	7	688	9	728	5
409	5	449	1	489	3	529	8	569	1	609	6	649	8	689	4	729	9

To Consult the T'ai Hsüan by Casting Sticks

The use of milfoil stalks to consult the I Ching, or even the T'ai Hsüan, gives some clue as to the origin of divination by casting sticks. The particular plant which is almost regarded as sacred may be one of two related species, the artemisia, or mugwort, and the yarrow, which itself exists in a number of varieties; two botanical names have been offered to identify the plant used by I Ching purists: either the *achillea millefolium* or *ptarmica sibirica*. The latter name gives a clue to the plant's origins, and also suggests that the original practitioners of the I Ching were from Northern China or Turkestan.

So prevalent in Southern China is the practice of divination by bamboo slips that it can only be considered as significant that bamboo slips are not used.

In Nothern latitudes, however, yarrow is a common enough plant, while bamboo is a curiosity in sheltered gardens, or else, if growing wild, an escape from some exotic enclave.

Willow-wands may have been used at one time; there is, in Herodotus, a description of the Scythians divining by willow wands, and the methods would no doubt have been similar. But the willow does demand a fairly damp situation, while yarrow grows abundantly in meadows, on grassy banks, and throughout the vast grasslands of the Steppes. It may be encountered frequently in mid- and late summer along the banks of motorways. I once gathered a sufficient number of yarrow stalks from a single roundabout in a suburb of North London.

The reason why yarrow is so suitable for the purpose is that the stems, when dried, are woody, firm, and manoeuvrable, unlike the stems of other common plants such as cow-parsley, which are usually too friable when dried. It is a simple matter to run the plant stem through the fingers, remove the leaves, and retain a straight, firm, stalk.

The flowers bear a superficial resemblance to cow parsley and the other unbellifers, but they are almost instantly distinguishable from surrounding umbellifers by the creamier, whiter colour despite the occasional touch of pink. The other clues are their feathery leaves, and the fact that the individual flowers are daisy-like.

Choose upright plants which stand about four feet (1.2m) high, for it is necessary to cut stem lengths each about a foot (30cm) long. The taller plants may be able to yield two stems, but generally the taller plants will be straggly and twisted, and the stems not of the best quality. They turn woody, once stripped of their leaves, in a surprisingly short time, and still retain their greenness. (The left-over wood was probably dried and ground to make artemisia punk; see the Commentary to Shou 55 for a note on the connection between the I Ching and moxibustion.)

For completeness, the following comments are based on the instructions given in the K'uei Pi I Ching on the traditional way to consult the I Ching. The publication issued by the Shun Chen Tang (Perfection of Goodness College) is of comparitively recent date (late Ch'ing dynasty) although obviously based on a much earlier work, but possibly not earlier than the Ming.*

These extra notes, it must be stressed, are given for background reference only, and are included for the reasons given by a former eminent sinologist, Professor Herbert Chatley: '. . . By thoroughly fixing the mind by ritual, fumigation and environment, the sortilege is carried out in a state of ecstasy which ensures that the process is either subconscious or controlled by spirits.'

Preamble

A special room should be reserved for the purpose of consulting the oracle; uncluttered, so that the mind is not distracted. It should open to the south.

A special table, about 3 ft(1m)×5 ft(1.5m) is necessary for the manipulations. The stalks should be kept in a special case, about 3 inches (7cm) in diameter. The height of the case is about half the length of the stalks, so that they do not fall out. (The text also adds that the box should be wrapped in red silk, and the whole kept in a black bag.)

On the table is placed a wooden frame, in the form of a board with legs. The board has holes where the stalks are placed during the manipulations. (The reason for this will be made clearer during the description of how the manipulations are carried out.) A censer is placed to the south of the frame.

When about to divine, cleanse and sweep the room. Prepare the ink-stone, water, brushes and ink, and have a yellow lacquer board ready east of the censer, for recording the results of the manipulations. Divination is made to the north. If necessary there can be an assistant.

The stalks are removed from the bag and fumigated in the censer; a prayer is offered for the success of the divination, and the determination of the mystical numbers begins.

At the close of the determination of the numbers, the implements are carefully returned to their proper places; incense is burnt once more, the diviner and the assistant do reverence and salute each other, and retire.

*Out of interest, the name K'uei Pi is that of two Chinese constellations (in the vicinity of Pisces) that were associated with the birth of some great sage or teacher.

The Manipulation of the Yarrow Stalks

The following reconstruction of the method of consulting the T'ai Hsüan will determine the four lines of the tetragram. In the T'ai Hsüan there are no 'moving' lines, because the T'ai Hsüan was not a book of changes. Instead, the Tsan is determined as a division of the Shou itself.

64 stalks are taken.

Separate the stalks at random into 3 bundles.

Take the first bundle (that is, the one on the RIGHT) and count out the stalks by 3's. There will be a remainder of 1, 2, or 0 stalks. Put these stalks to one side; if there is no remainder, take a stalk from *the bundle which has just been dealt* and put this at one side instead.

Take the middle bundle. Again count it out by 3's; put the remainder together with the remainder from the first bundle. If there is no remainder, take a stalk from the bundle and add it to the previous remainder (or extra stalk, if there was no remainder).

Take up the third bundle (the one on the LEFT) and again count it out by 3's. Again, put the remainder with the other remainders, or if there is no remainder, take a stalk and add it to them.

Count the number of stalks in the remainder pile.

There will be three, four, or five stalks.

(For some reason, although one stalk is added to the pile whether or not the remainder was 1 or 0, the number of stalks in the remainder pile determines how many times no remainder was left when the bundles were counted out.)

If the number of stalks in the remainder pile is 3 then there was one remainder of One, and this signifies T'ien.

The bottom, or Chia line, of the Shou can now be written as T'ien, and is written as an unbroken line, ▬▬.

If the number of stalks in the remainder pile is 4, then there would have been one remainder of Two in the manipulations.

Two is the number of Jen, and therefore the bottom line is written as a singly broken line, ▬ ▬.

If the number of stalks in the remainder pile is 5, this indicates that there was one remainder of Three. Three is the number of Ti; and the bottom line of the Shou is written as a line broken into three, ▪ ▪ ▪

The stalks are now all gathered together, and the whole process repeated three more times in order to determine the remaining lines of the Shou.

Determining the Tsan

Take up all the stalks, remove one, and place it to one side.

Again, divide the stalks into 3 bundles, the first bundle on the *right*.

Take the left-hand and the central bundles, and put them together.

Divide them into 3, and put the right handle little bundle with the original right hand bundle.

Again, take the left-hand and central bundles, put them together, and divide into three. Put the right hand little bundle with the original right hand bundle.

Repeat once again, so that the original right hand bundle now has 3 additional sub-bundles added to it.

Take the right hand bundle, and count out by nines. The remainder is the number of the Tsan.

Determining the Tsan from the 729 Hexagrams

There is yet one more method of determining the Tsan, which is to consider them as being arrangements of 729 hexagrams (six-lined diagrams), divided into threes, thus:

1 365 729

If the number of lines in the diagrams is increased to five, then the total number of diagrams possible (when the lines are divided into threes) becomes 273; when increased to six, the number of permutations possible is 729, thus accommodating each of the Tsan.

To consult the T'ai Hsüan Ching by six-lined hexagrams, it is necessary to increase the number of casts of the stalks to six, using the first part of the method described above.

The number of the Tsan may be calculated quite simply. The top four lines of the hexagram represents the Shou; the lower two the division of the Shou into Tsan as follows:

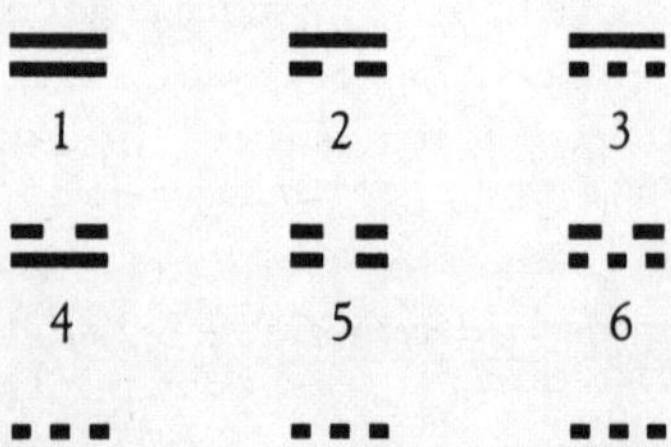

The Tsan Texts

As has been explained in the Introduction to the T'ai Hsüan Ching, although standard editions of the work show the text divided into Tsan, it is by no means certain that these divisions are in fact by Yang Hsiung. The problem is therefore, having found the Shou which encompasses the relevant Tsan number, knowing what parts of the Shou text pertain to that particular Tsan. If the texts had been pointed up to show any conjectural divisions, this edition would have fallen into the same errors as those earlier versions which masked Yang Hsiung's text with lengthy glosses. In order to leave the texts as uncluttered as possible, a discreet approach has been made to this problem.

In the lengthier texts, where division into Tsan is a relatively obvious matter, numbers have been placed at the sides of the verses to indicate likely relationships with the Tsan divisions. Very often, the opening (and sometimes other) verses are relevant to all the Tsan within that Shou. The rule is, therefore, that *all unnumbered verses apply to all the Tsan within that Shou.*

In other cases, where the Shou texts are so obviously continuous that it would be wrong to break up the text, or where the text contains no oracle verses (as in, for example, Shou 67) a divination aspect can be elicited from the Lo Shu (Magic Square of Nine Numbers), applied to the numerology of the 729 Tsan. This can be done simply by referring to the list of Tsan Aspects, and cross-refer to the diagram of the Lo Shu for the meaning.

When there is no Tsan text, the whole of the Shou text applies to each Tsan, the meaning modified by the aspect given by the Lo Shu.

Nevertheless, it is advisable to read the whole of the Shou text to gain an insight into the context, whether the Tsan are marked or not.

Good and evil are shown
By the four stars of the Plough

A sash fastened by a hook hangs down
And passes through the hole of a jade ring.
Shou 2

PART TWO:
THE SHOU

Shou 1
Tsan 1-9
CHUNG
The Centre

中

Active flux
Latent sprouting

In the Yellow Palace
There is nothing that is not.
Is not this the Secret, thus? *1*

The Mind makes war against the Secret
Which can explain both Yin and Yang. *2/2*

The Dragon issues from the Centre
The Head and Tail are signs revealing
How it will be used. *3-5/3-5*

The Treasury is empty;
Therefore the great are denied life. *6/6*

The Sun is Chief in Heaven;
By fortune are the seasons ordered. *7/7*

The Moon's watch is extensive;
Unlike the West's enlightenment. *8/8*

Yellow is not yellow;
Back and forth goes the Autumn routine. *9/9*

中

Notes

As is the case with nearly every Shou, the number of 'divination' verses is considerably fewer than nine, the number of Tsan to each Shou. In this instance there are five, not counting the opening formula which is a standard opening for almost all the first forty Shou. (This is of significant importance in, for example, Shou 3, Hsien, q.v.) The following phrase, a 'philosophical statement' clearly refers to the T'ai Hsüan's use as a calendar, and describes the Winter season, when life is in seed, and has not yet made its appearance. Yang Hsiung likens this to Chung itself: it is the seed from which all the other Shou sprout. The Dragon (of cosmological significance) is also regarded as being generated from the Centre, Chung.

In the third verse, Yang Hsiung is saying that the T'ai Hsüan may puzzle the reader, but that eventually the evidence of one's own eyes will show the superiority of the T'ai Hsüan over other accepted philosophies, whether, in Yang Hsiung's time, the Principle of Duality, or in modern times, the accepted laws of science and mathematics.

With regards to the divination texts, note that 'Sun' and 'Moon' also mean 'Day' and 'Month' in Chinese; while this has no relevance to the text here, it may be an important symbolism for someone using the verses for a prognostication.

The final verse contains a type of construction which occurs several times through the T'ai Hsüan: 'A is not A' (for further examples, see Shou 5 and 25). In '*Researches on the I Ching*', the only other work in a European language to quote the T'ai Hsüan extensively, I. K. Shchutskii links the statement with the final couplet, and translates it as 'yellow *does not* yellow' in the sense of the yellowing of autumnal leaves; this is not my opinion, for reasons outlined in the introduction, page 23. That this is Shchutskii's translation from the Chinese, and not the translator's version of Shchutskii, is clear from the Russian text: 'Zheltoye nye zheltoyet' instead of 'Zhelto nye zhelto'. Yellow is an imperial colour (see the second couplet); for example 'yellow metal' means 'gold' in Chinese. Yellow is also the colour of 'Earth' in the five-element system.

The final character of this Shou, translated here as 'routine' but which also means regulations, habits, and frequency, is the title of Shou 51.

Further remarks on the divinatory meaning and symbolism of 'Chung' will be found in an earlier work of the author (*Your Future Revealed by the Mah Jongg*: Aquarian Press, 1982).

Shou 2
Tsan 10-18
CHOU
Surrounding

周

Active flux
Surrounding the mind;
And also returning.

Does not the creation of things
Begin by assembling them into groups?

Rewards are in the heart of Heaven;
Consider virtue;
Whether it be so, or if it be not so. 1/10

Plants are the central pivot
Without which the world outside would gasp for breath. 2/11

It leaves me.
It enters me. 3/12

Good and evil are shown
By the four stars of the Plough. 4/13

A sash fastened by a hook hangs down
And passes through the hole of a jade ring. 5/14

A humble cottage — Gold — A warning:
The poor do not have the means. 6/15

The token of CHOU is honesty
Which ascends and perfumes Heaven. 7/16

Eyes blind to shameful actions
See their friends rewarded
By their being unable to inspire allegiance. 8/17

Rewards for journeys outside one's body;
Such calamities are not great. 9/18

周

Notes

What an astonishing wealth of symbolism and philosophy leaps from these few lines! The first two verses can be understood to refer to the forces which bind the particles of atoms together; hydrogen is the simplest atom; in the creation of the universe, all atoms were generated from these simplest atoms.

Another aspect of natural science is touched upon in verses four and five — how could Yang Hsiung have known, in 10 BC, that plants, by photosynthesis, breathe out the oxygen vital for animal life? 'It leaves me, it enters me'. Does this refer to breath — the oxygen that leaves plants, and enters the animals, both of them living creatures, signified by Chou?

The 'four stars of the plough' refers to the four stars which make up the body of the 'Northern Ladle' Pei Tou (北斗) which points to the Pole Star, symbol of virtue.

The word K'uei (魁) can however also mean one specific star, and in this sense is the ruling deity of that constellation; and also, by extension, the patron deity of literature. The verse can therefore also be interpreted 'Good and Evil are revealed by the (spirit of) Literature'; the knowledge of good and evil; discernment through learning.

Several verses refer to the rewards offered by Heaven for virtuous behaviour, but the last verse is very mysterious. I doubt if it refers to astral projection, although the character means physical body, not personality. Perhaps it can be interpreted more clearly in the light of the questions put to the T'ai Hsüan. There are two purely omen verses; the one regarding the cottage (that is, a poor man's house) and the image of the sash (signifying honour) fastened through a jade ring (even greater honour).

'Chou' is the name of the dynasty which preceeded the Han (when the T'ai Hsüan was written) and 'Chou I' 周 易 meaning 'The [book of] Changes of the Chou' is the name usually given to the I Ching by academics. Similarly, 'Chung' is often used to mean China, its people, or its language.

The character for 'eyes blind' in the penultimate verse is the title of Shou 68, Meng.

Shou 3
Tsan 19-27
HSIEN
Slowly

礥

Active flux.

Subtly moving, moving,
And so slowly, slowly,
Life's difficulties begin.

Yellow is pure;
In secret. Unseen, its boundaries conceal
The flourishing by the fountain. 1/9

Yellow is not pure;
It submits to the source. 2/20

Crimson:
The Son supports, supports; 3/21

The chief omen indicates finality. 4/22

Uprooting me; no virtue in
Using force but not skill. 5/23

Pulling out the carriage
Mountain and abyss,
Appropriately for the highly placed person. 6/24

Lofty, lofty, high exalted mountain.
At its foot are rivers, breakers. 7/25

Men must navigate those waters.
If they row in harmony
They can pass over easily. 8/26

Great exalted mountain;
River unharmoniously navigated,
No skill there. 9/27

礥

Notes

The opening words of this section are quoted in the K'ang Hsi dictionary to illustrate the title character of this Shou, Hsien (礥) slowly and laboriously, which is rare, even in classical usage. It is re-quoted in Giles' dictionary, with the translation 'When the breath of Spring gently moves, movement slowly begins'. Unfortunately, this translation takes into account the opening two characters, Yang Ch'i (陽 氣) which begin most of the first forty Shou, and which can therefore be regarded as independent of the rest of the text.

The Shou corresponds to the first week in January, and could not therefore be readily regarded as belonging to a period when the 'breath of Spring' would be gently moving. Rather, 'unseen' is the germination of the earliest plants of the year, perhaps the yellow crocus. The final character of the opening verse is the same as the title of Shou 79 (Difficulties). It cannot be a coincidence that Shou 79 is the third from the end, the counterpart of this one.

'Yellow' is the colour of the Earth, 'crimson' (fiery red) the colour of the fire element.

Here, all the verses are prognostications, of greater or lesser obscurity, which the diviner must interpret in the light of the question and the surrounding circumstances.

There are frequent references to 'mountain' and 'abyss' throughout the T'ai Hsüan, and these no doubt are references to the ups and down of life; the peaks and troughs of one's biorhythms perhaps! The significance of 'abyss' is dealt with in the prefatory chapter.

The contradictions between pairs of verses applies, of course, to the particular Tsan which prevails in the reading of the Shou.

'The chief omen' is the literal meaning of two characters Yuan Chen, which are part of the opening formula, or standard magical incantation, of the I Ching, and as such these characters are virtually untranslatable.

Shou 4
Tsan 28-36
HSIEN
A Barrier

Active flux.
A barrier to Yin;
Slowly, surely.

Things completing
See the closing.

The snake bows to the mud. *1/28*

Without the cock, the hen will die.
No one bestows gifts. *2/29*

HSIEN is the concealing and embedding of precious stones. *3/30*

The toll-gate lacks a bolt;
Put aside the golden key. *4/31*

HSIEN [*Shou 3*] means 'slowly';
HSIEN [*Shou 4*] means 'a barrier'. *5/32*
Uprooting my villainy and evil;
Stone may grind stone. *6/33*

Weakly, weakly, are the barriers closed;
Hurry to remove doubt
From the conscience of the inferior. *7/34*

Crimson, stinking,
Banished from the frontier,
He fearfully enters the house. *8/35*

By closing the gate
The conclusion is empty. *9/36*

閑

Notes

The numerous cross-references to the previous Shou are due no doubt to the fact that the two Shou have identical pronunciations. The second verse may be a reference to the thirty-first hexagram of the I Ching. Apart from the first two verses, the entire text is of a prognosticatory character. 'Stone grinds stone' (or diamond cut diamond) can be taken as 'grinding cruelty'.

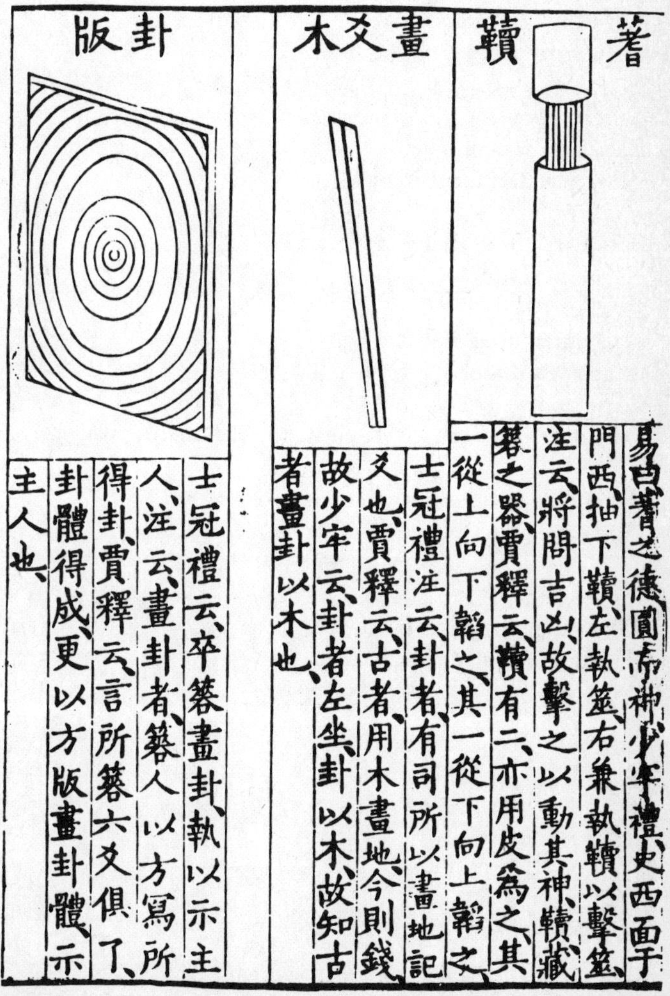

Shou 5
Tsan 37-45
SHAO
The Least

Active flux.
Quietly surely,
Showing in the dark abyss.

The element of congealing;
Thus, it can make itself
A flaming aloe.

Poverty, poverty,
False rumours of relief;
No protection for the chief. 1/37 2/38

The Earth itself dashes down
In the torrents. 3/39

The Earth itself dashes down
Man's latest idols. 4/40 5/41

The poor man himself examines the rich man's presents. 6/42

Poverty is not poverty;
Someone plans relief. 7/43 8/44

Quiet rains;
The valleys begin to shoot.
Humility is quietude. 9/45

少

Notes

The Earth Self is a reference to the 'Ti' of the three parts of the T'ai Hsüan. The tetragram for SHAO has two unbroken lines (T'ien) and two 'Jen' lines, but no 'Ti'. It is therefore dominated totally and equally by active and zero forces. The lack of 'Jen' lines explains the violent symbolism of the 'Earth Self' verses.

The 'aloe' is a plant which suddenly burst into bloom, with showy and unexpectedly enormous flower heads. The variety mentioned in the text is the *allium odorum* (I have added the word 'flaming' for the sake of euphony, and to try to point up the symbolism). Ch'en Jen Hsi's notes suggest that this verse means 'Humility is its own reward' by offering an alternative reading for aloe.

The omens refer to poverty, and assistance from outside sources.

Note that the title of the Shou, SHAO, the Least, is never once mentioned in the text.

Shou 6
Tsan 46-54
LI
Tribulations

戾

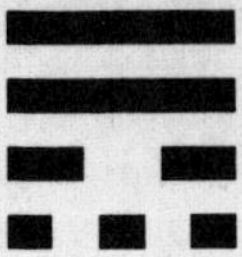

Active flux.
Hatching tiny things
Each crafty pair;
And butting against each other
Every kind and species.

Tribulations in the entrails;
The Chief turns his back on the Centre;
Outside are contentions. *1/46*

In the South East, shooting forth:
The she-rhinoceros.
In the North West, an arrow. *2/47 3/48*

The draughtsman's compasses,
The carpenter's square,
The water-level and plumb-line;
No similarities are manifested. *4/49 5/50*

Killing and begetting
Are mutual arrows.
Central Harmony is the Way. *6/51 7/52*

The granary of intelligence for the hen.
Unlike the lodging place of the oriole. *8/53*

To err in law, a year's merit and skill. *9/54*

Notes

Apart from the opening verse, which refers to the natural events of the pre-Spring season, most of the text is of a mystical character. The she-rhinoceros, Ssu (兕), is not the beast that one might encounter in zoological gardens, but a mythical creature, the female of some kind of single or triple-horned buffalo. The light of its burning horn enabled one to see the creatures when looking into deep, dark, waters. This animal's mate is the Hsi, and the two are illustrated on page 132. It will be seen that neither creature remotely resembles a rhinoceros, although one of them may have some slight familiarity with the unicorn of Western legend. Apart from the colours of the two creatures, notice the feet. The Ssu appears again in Shou 43.

In the same verse, the 'shooting forth' is the same character as that used to mean the shooting forth of plants in the abyss, in the previous Shou. There are other cross-references in this text which unfortunately it is not easy to show in translation; but it is perhaps important to note that the 'oriole' of the penultimate verse is the same as the mating birds in the opening verse. It is also the character for the name of the thirtieth hexagram of the I Ching, where it is usually translated as 'Brightness'.

As in English, the word 'arrow' has both the significance of a missile and a direction pointer.

Compare the fourth verse with the third verse of Shou 29; the craftsmen's instruments in this verse are associated with the elements, colours, trades, and ministries as follows:

Compasses: Wood, Green, Agriculture.

Carpenter's square: Metal, White, Justice.

Plumb line: Earth, Yellow, the State.

The meaning of the last two verses was a complete enigma until it was realized that the imagery is astrological. According to Ch'en Jen Hsi, the 'granary of intelligence' is the T'ai Sui, or Year Star — the planet Jupiter. This, by its twelve-yearly orbit of the heavens reckons the twelve years of the Great Cycle, now more popularly known by such names as rat, ox, tiger and the like. The 'hen' is the Metal planet, Venus, also called the Great White, T'ai Peh. By 'lodging-place' or Hsiu is meant one of the lunar mansions. The text of the latter verses is therefore a very abstruse allusion to a conjunction of Venus and Jupiter in the same lunar mansion, and the portents which are deduced therefrom.

Shou 7
Tsan 55-63
SHANG
Top (Ascent)

上

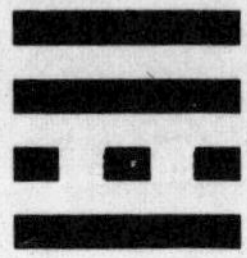

Active flux.
The birth of things from the foundations,
Shooting forth together from the Earth,
Then rising gradually upwards to the top.

At the top, purity.
The heart grinds on, engraving, engraving. *1/55*

The clacking of cranes ascends:
The Self mounts the ancient stairway
Heaven's dictates do not have reasons. *2/56 3/57*

The ascent to the meeting place,
Clothes in disarray, fine garments slashed.
The traveller is not congratulated. *4/58-6/60*

The ascent is dangerous;
The ladder axed;
The loss of scholarly people. *7/61-9/63*

上

Notes

SHANG is a very common word meaning both 'top' and 'to ascend'. Since the text uses several words to mean rising and ascending, I have used the word 'top' only where the character (上) occurs.

The Crane is a symbol of longevity; another word for ancient, long-living, occurs in the same verse; this renders the verse more comprehensible — it is a reference to a long and respected life.

The remainder of the text, of a prognosticatory character, is surprisingly unambiguous.

Shou 8
Tsan 64-72
KAN (*CH'IEN*)
To oppose (*A Thousand*)

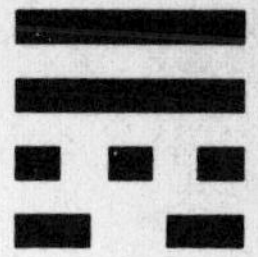

Active flux
Supporting things
Is this not also piercing through?

Resistant matter; sounds of creaking;
Then burning; boring through. 1/64-3/66

Opposing words; (*A thousand words*)
Entering the bones. 4/67-6/69

Opposing, opposing, (*A thousand thousand*)
Drifting clouds fall from Heaven. 7/70-9/72

Notes
In this short text, the only difficulty lies in the title of the Shou itself. In all editions of the text it is clearly KAN (干) meaning 'to oppose'. However, this character is very similar to the character Ch'ien (千) meaning 'a thousand' and it may be that the brief text makes more sense when interpreted this way. I offer the alternative reading where KAN occurs.

Shou 9
Tsan 73-81
SHU
Penetrating

Active flux
Strong inside but weak outside.

Things completed support the penetrating;
Also entering, the just and great.

We ourselves, defer to authority and show respect.
Excellence is equivalent to appropriateness and virtue;
Deferring to authority and showing respect
Is appropriate and virtuous.
Suppose that such actions were lacking! *1/73-3/75*

Penetrating from drink and food brings plumpness.
There is no flattery. *4/76-6/78*

Broad daylight now at nine o'clock;
Possibilities by way of a servant:
One who can hear. *7/79-9/81*

Notes

First, the name of the Shou: SHU may mean 'penetrating' as it has been translated here, or else 'broadcasting', in the sense of sowing seed. But note the link between the title of this Shou and the text of the previous one, which has many references to boring and penetration.

Another curious point, which may have no significance, is the fact that the tetragram has a resemblance to the character (示) Shih, meaning an omen. Because of this, it is worth looking at the character for this Shou, which includes the radical (爻) meaning one of the diagrams of the I Ching. (Also see Shou 55 for a further reference to this radical.)

This short text contains one of several little homilies on virtuous behaviour which occur throughout the T'ai Hsüan. (There is a further note in the commentary to Shou 12.)

Wu Wang, first ruler of the Chou Dynasty (after which the Chou I, or Book of Changes of the Chou Dynasty, takes its name) consulting the tortoise carapace and milfoil stalks. See Shou 12, 50, etc.

Mistakes in divining by the milfoil stalks;
In the tortoise is property emerging from the mud.
Shou 12

Shou 10
Tsan 82-90
HSIEN
Praise

Active flux
Assisting the concealed to slough their wrappings.

Assisting the living, but not yet active,
To acquire just habits. 1/82

Admiring the judgements
Of upright and fortunate men. 2/83

Not fortuitous.
Great falsehoods
Since the deflection. 3/84 4/85

Perhaps honesty, perhaps the wing of a bird,
Points out the sage. 5/86

False are those ancient distortions;
The gentle are beginning by the gossip of the cruel. 6/87 7/88

The carriage axle bends;
The shaft breaks off.
Four horses thereupon are trapped. 8/89

The nobleman spits blood. 9/90

Notes

The only observation is that the first character after the opening formula 'Yang Ch'i' is Tsan, Assisting, which is the term Yang Hsiung uses to refer to the sub-divisions of the Shou.

'Spits blood' means 'slanders'; here are three references to false doctrines. A further reference to the team of four horses appears in Shou 28.

Shou 11
Tsan 91-99
CH'A
To mistake

差

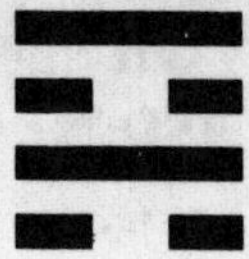

Active flux.
Wriggling, it splits open.

In the East, the Supreme cause.
Multitudes in harmony;
The element CH'A to mistake
Its appearance.

Letting go produces that which is good;
Holding on produces that which is evil. *1/91*

They perish, they perish,
Trying to reach that radiant brightness. *2/92 3/93*

Passing through the gate, are broken off.
Entering, to reach that other Centre. *4/94*

In going, the Great stumble passing through that gate;
Do not enter that house. *5/95*

Feet are bound, are bound.
His steps staggering. *6/96*

The boots . . . the cart shafts . . .
Engraving destroyed by fire . . . the tailless deer. *7/97 8/98*

Passing through that charred city,
A tree-stump there, perhaps is green, is green. *9/99*

差

Notes

As it stands, the penultimate verse is meaningless. There are, however, links between the two verses either side of it. The boots which begin the verse latch on to the imagery of the stumbling feet in previous verses; the destruction by fire of an engraved object ties in with the picture of the charred city, in which only a tree stump remains with the prospect of renewed life. The tailless deer, however, does not seem to relate to anything else, but this is not unusual in the text of the T'ai Hsüan — we have already encountered such sudden images: visionary flashes of a she-rhinoceros, ten thousand goblets, and the like.

There are two distinct sets of images in this text; the first few verses refer to the hatching of some kind of creature, trying to attain the sun, and being scorched in the process. In the second half of the text, we have the image of a great personage stumbling as he passes through a gate, and a city destroyed by fire, like the creatures tyring to reach the sun. Compare this text with the text of Shou 4, a Barrier.

'In the East, the Supreme cause' must refer to the sun; but the meaning of 'that other Centre' in the fifth verse is open to any amount of conjecture. It is something which will probably reveal itself to the questioner in the light of his personal circumstances.

'His steps staggering' can also mean 'a slip of the tongue.' The disjointed text of the eighth verse has been interpreted by Ch'en Jen Hsi as a sense of portents; for example 'boots' means urgent business; 'cart-shafts', look to the future, or, look up; 'tailless deer', fawning flattery. (This last also appears in the next Shou, 12). 'Green' in the last verse, is the associated colour of the 'wood' element.

Shou 12
Tsan 100-108
T'UNG
The young boy.

童

Active flux.
Beginning to pry,

The element T'UNG, the young boy,
Surely completed,
Does not yet have the knowledge. *1/100*

Mistakes in divining by the milfoil stalks;
In the tortoise is property emerging from the mud. *2/101 3/102*

Entering wealth,
In the East, at early morning,
The light is not enough to go by. *4/103 5/104*

The great raising of the curtain screens,
By which the visitor is shown direction. *6/105*

Long the pigmy, pigmy,
Studies with the Crimson Sage. *7/106 8/107*

T'UNG, the tailless deer butting their heads;
Cottage ashes are this Head. *9/108*

童

Notes

Several points need elucidation here. The young boy, T'UNG, the name of this Shou, may be the young boy (referred to in the text) of the fourth hexagram of the I Ching, Meng, often translated as 'Youthful Inexperience'. In fact, as will be seen in the notes to Shou 50, The Dodder, the boy may perhaps be a shaman's apprentice, sent out to collect mystical herbs. Further evidence of this is in the text: 'Does not yet have knowledge' immediately calls to mind the 'Youthful Inexperience' of the I Ching.

This image is picked up in the next verse, which refers to errors in carrying out the lengthy and complex process of calculating the lines of the hexagrams of the I Ching. The other standard means of divination in ancient China was by tortoise carapace — since the less wealthy made do with shoulder blades of sacrificed animals, the employment of tortoise carapaces must have indicated wealth: property emerging from the mud.

'Early morning' is how I have translated the fifth hour of the daily cycle, 7am-9am. The 'brightness' in the East is the reason why the traveller is unable to set off; in Shou 9 (corresponding to a fortnight earlier) it was already broad daylight at that hour. The significance seems to be that the traveller ought to have set off before daybreak.

The 'Crimson (or vermilion) Sage' was the name for a dwarf who was supposed to eat cinnabar (the red oxide of mercury, a highly toxic substance) which not only prolonged his life, but turned base metals into gold. (Rubbing base metals with mercury compounds can give them a silvery shine, which may be the origin of this fable.) Prolonging his years would of course give him opportunity to study and acquire wisdom.

The tailless deer of the previous Shou appears again here. This particular creature was reputed to flee from its own reflection in the water — a symbol of timidity, but here the deer are duelling.

The final character 'Head' refers not only to the head of the deer, but to this text — the word Shou 首 having the meaning 'head'.

Chou Kung, younger brother of Wu Wang, consulting the tortoise carapaces.

Shou 13
Tsan 109-117
TSENG
Increase

增

Active flux.
Luxuriant growth increasing;
This shows things daily fattening
Imperceptibly prospering.

Hear the Oracle!
TSENG increasing in the darkness:
Outside, men are not achieving. *1/109*

Hear the Oracle!
TSENG increasing in the darkness:
Inside, it is distinct. *2/110*

There is no increase;
It is the direction. *3/111*

There is increase;
It is light in the darkness. *4/112*

A low-lying marsh
Signifies a crowd of people
Glistening, altogether. *5/113*

TSENG is the nobleman;
A knife is scratching something out. *6/114*

TSENG, the nobleman's knife,
Is scratching out;
There are disadvantages accompanying actions. *7/115*

The precipitous heights
Do not fall in ruins: *8/116*

Rely on those other hills
Either side of the chasm. *9/117*

Shou 14
Tsan 118-126
JUI
Sharpness

Active flux.
The Summit.
By sharpness things are brought to life,
Completed, and scattered abroad.

One is;
But not two. *1/118*

Sharpness is East,
Forgetfulness is West. *2/119*

To see what is behind
And not see what is in the heart. *3/120*

Sharpness in ugliness:
Holding in the mouth five cartloads. *4/121 5/122*

Ten thousand goblets:
An auspicious omen. *6/123*

Sharpness in ugliness:
Good fortune;
The salary proferred is not measured. *7/124 8/125*

Sharpness in advantage:
Disgrace and evil attainments. *9/126*

銳

Notes

This almost exclusively prognosticatory text needs very little explanation. 'Sharpness' here means 'sharpness of mind'; the omens are favourable when there is 'sharpness in ugliness' but unfavourable when there is 'sharpness in advantage'. This can be taken to mean that one should be able to see hidden value in something which is outwardly unattractive — inner beauty, perhaps. Conversely, only being able to see good in something which has material advantage will lead to evil.

For further references to the mathematical reasoning arising out of the statement 'One is, but not two' see page 194. The constituent lines of the tetragram give a clue to this unambiguous equation: an unbroken line is supported by three bisected ones — T'ien, supported by three Jen.

The 'auspicious omen' of the fifth verse is Chen (貞), one of the omen formulae of the I Ching; it is the fourth character of the opening line of the text, and frequently occurs thereafter. It is usually translated as 'auspicious' although it can also mean 'to inquire by divination' as well as being a technical term for the lower of the two trigrams forming the I Ching hexagram.

The opening flowers of the first verse are in accordance with a temperate climate: this Shou covers February 18-22.

Shou 15
Tsan 127-135
TA
Perceiving

達

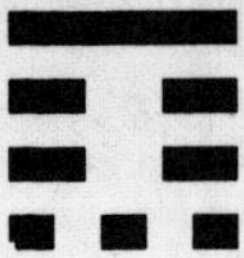

Active flux.
Twigs and branches emerging;
All things, all matter, perceiving (*making itself known*).

The Central darkness, alone perceiving,
Distant, distant, not submitting. *1/127*

The Central darkness, alone perceiving,
Inner dawn, lacking direction. *2/128*

Deceive the thighs,
Perceive the eyes. *3/129*

Green trees bind streams;
Their beauty may, by perceiving,
Be like the plumping of a gourd. *4/130 5/131*

Green trees bind streams,
Inner judgements and consideration. *6/132*

Little advantage;
Little perceiving, great deceiving. *7/133*

Tombstones, tombstones,
Not preserving. *8/134*

Perceiving (*making known*), though hacked in stone,
Perishes; afterwards, false records. *9/135*

逢

Notes

This is one of a handful of Shou in which there must be doubt regarding the actual title of the Shou itself. Different readings of the title are not confined to different editions of the work; in the same edition a different character is used for the heading to that which appears in the table of contents, and a possible third reading in a poem at the end of the T'ai Hsüan which summarizes the attributes of the Shou. Matters are further complicated by similar characters appearing in the text, as if even the old editors were not sure which of the characters in the text was intended as the heading. Fortunately it is sometimes possible to guess at the meaning intended (given a choice of possibilities) because verses throughout the T'ai Hsüan often compare and contrast ideas with the use of synonymous and antonymous phrases. This has led here to the reading 'perceiving' though for the sake of completeness the alternative reading 'crossroads' is offered. This could, for example, be a possible reading in the third verse, where there is the idea of 'lacking direction'.

'Deceive the thighs . . .' I have retained the image of 'thighs' here, for reasons which I have given in the preface, although the word is a loan for 'division'. 'Fraudulent division is perceived' is the intended meaning.

'Green trees' is used in place of 'green wood' (that is, saplings, etc.) since although this is a possible calendrical reference to the sap rising into the leaves, the ancient text has the commentary 'Trees bear their branches by means of their roots' which is probably a reference to family, ancestors and progeny. Conversely, the gourd does not 'plump' until the Autumn (as the poet Keats tells us in his Ode), but the expression actually refers to growing children, not the vegetable.

'Tombstones' is a convenient translation of 'Pien' which means an ancestral memorial tablet. The meaning here is quite clear: even records graven on stone do not last for ever.

Shou 16
Tsan 136-144
CHIAO
Exchange

交

Yang is exchanged for Yin,
Yin is exchanged for Yang.
Matter ascends.

The Bright Assembly Hall:
Deliberations, deliberations.
Excellence, excellence. *1/136*

Exchanging wood for stone:
Impossible are man's inclinations. *2/137 3/138*

Departing; returning black.
Blackness and the spirit exchange elements. *4/139 5/140*

Exchange the oriole for the ape
Not caught in hunting for their glory. *6/141*

The Great Circle is wide, wide.
The Little Circle is exchanged for it. *7/142 8/143*

I have spiritual food
Together with your food. *9/144*

交

Notes

This is the first text which does not begin with 'Yang Ch'i', active flux, the character Ch'i, breath, current, flux, being omitted in the opening phrase. The Ming Tang (Bright Assembly Hall) was part of the Imperial Temple, used for sacrifices to the High God, and also where the Emperor held audience with the feudal princes.

There is a reference here to the 'five element' theory, specifically the interchange of the five materials wood, stone, water, metal, and fire, although only two are mentioned. Although the Chinese Five Elements bore the names of material things (excepting, of course, fire) the 'elements' were not so much the things themselves but the forces which bound them together. The exchanging of these forces could therefore be described as the exchanging of two opposite forces. When a battery is used to operate a lamp or some other contrivance, there is an exchange of chemical processes in the battery which causes the flow, or Ch'i, of the electric current through the apparatus. Black is the colour associated with the element 'water'. The Great Circle must refer to the Celestial Sphere, since Heaven was regarded as round, but the Earth as a square.

The character for 'Exchange' is of particular interest: the upper part of the character is similar to the character for 'six' and the lower part is similar to the (乂) of Yao (爻), meaning one of the (six) lines of the hexagrams.

The 'oriole' is more properly the 'mango-bird', and similarly 'ape' should be 'orang outang'.

Shou 17
Tsan 145-153
JUAN
Soft

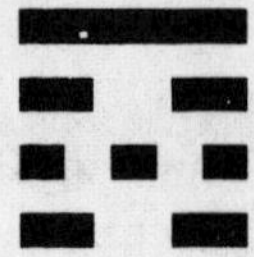

Active flux.
Can be hard; can be soft;
Can be active; can be at rest.

Seeing difficulties, draws in its coils. *1/145*

Now there is a boat;
Its direction is sharpness. *2/146*

Advantage in advancing
By retreating. *3/147*

Softness in the heart makes sickness;
Softness in the mind is a guardian. *4/148*

It is a symbol: supposing, therefore,
That the end should lack opposition? *5/149 6/150*

Yellow mushrooms do not bear children
As soon as there is a gap in the clouds. *7/151*

Yellow mushrooms do not bear children:
Clothing for a couple. *8/152*

The arrow points to a season of doubt;
Inheriting calamities. *9/153*

耎

Notes

The second verse refers to Shou 14.

In the fourth verse, 'flexibility' is a more appropriate translation, but the same translation has been retained for each appearance of the character 'JUAN'.

See the cross-reference in Shou 73.

Shou 18
Tsan 154-162
HSI
Waiting

徯

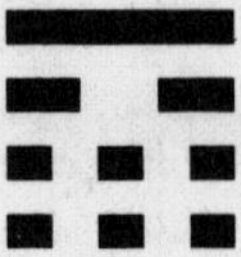

Active flux:
There is waiting.

Possibilities by means of penetrating,
And things which penetrate completely,
To achieve desires. *1/154*

Great ranks gather together
In the palace harmoniously;
The humble man in lowly cottage
Waits empty-handed. *2/155 3/156*

Waiting: Prosperity: An auspicious omen.
An auspicious omen: food and gold. *4/157 5/158 6/159*

Waiting: Misfortune: Insignificant trifles.
Insignificant trifles: evil.
A scoundrel's lodgings. *7/160 8/161*

No calamity, calamity in waiting;
Heaven unites us. *9/162*

The royal carriage, pulled by a team of four horses. (Shou 10 and 28).

Time: 7.
Time: 9.
The carriage rolls along its way.
Shou 28

Shou 19
Tsan 163-171
TS'UNG
Compliance

從

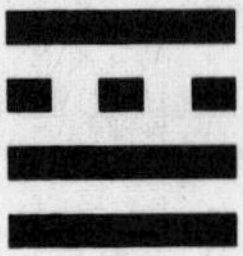

Yang skips in the abyss,
In the marshes, in the fields,
On the mountain peaks.
Things stand on tiptoe,
On the points of their feet.

The man who does not attack:
Himself will draw compliance. *1/163*

The man who does not attack;
He will surely be his own defence. *2/164*

Compliance of water
Is a series of aqueducts. *3/165*

Compliance of water, being a series of aqueducts,
Does not overflow itself. *4/166*

Compliance in the eye;
Erring in the belly. *5/167*

Shake off such ugliness;
Compliance is in cleanliness. *6/168 7/169*

The Golden Cockerel eating meat. *8/170*

Compliance is honourable;
Honourable are the followers;
Thereupon mounting the ladder. *9/171*

從

Notes

'Yang skips in the abyss' may be a pun on the words Yang (陽) active flux, and Yang (羊) sheep; it might even be a third pun on Yang Hsiung's own name as well. This Shou is the beginning of the third of the nine yearly divisions corresponding to period covering March 12 to April 21, which in the Western calendar is the period when Easter is likely to fall; the description of skipping and frolicking fits exactly.

The only passage which gives concern here, and one which seems to have troubled early commentators, is the phrase which I have translated as 'The Golden Cockerel eating meat'. The adjective used is not 'golden' but yellow yet again; yellow is the colour of the Earth element. Nor is the bird in question (necessarily) a farmyard cockerel — the male of birds, unspecified, is all that is indicated.

Shou 20
Tsan 172-180
CHIN
Advancing

進

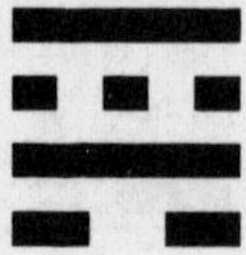

The active forces stretch out;
Indeed, advancing.

Things emerge from the mass;
The mass opens clearly,
Yet there are thorns. *1/172-3/174*

In obscurity advancing;
There is no action;
Yielding to the mother. *4/175-6/177*

If you go to the chapter,
The chapter is not reached.

The central path of the Sun,
Flies suspended over the darkness of Yin.
The myriad things in the universe melt.

Advancing through the abyss
The knight uses a boat. *7/178-9/180*

進

Notes

The 'myriad things' is a common expression used to mean 'everything in the universe'. 'Knight' is perhaps an awkward way of translating an expression which would have easily been understood a generation or two ago as 'a gentleman', but unfortunately both this word, and the concept, seem to be disappearing. Although the word 'knight' is used anachronistically, it does convey some of the sense of a person of chivalry, scholastic attainment, manners, and refinement. This Shou corresponds to the Spring Equinox. See the chapter on the calendar, page 33.

Shou 21
Tsan 181-189
SHIH
Release

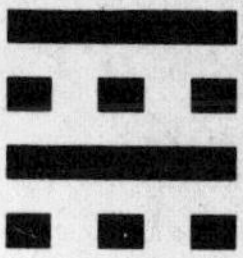

Active flux.
Harmoniously enlivening,
Gentle heat opens out all nature.

Taxes are manacles;
The taxed are released from their dues. *1/181*

The wind begins to shake,
The thunder increasing follows . . . *2/182 3/183*

The high exalted nobleman. *4/184*

Shaking, shaking,
Do not use insulting words;
Wash the mouth,
Cleanse it from shame. *5/185 6/186*

Shaking, shaking,
Do not use insulting words;
Releasing shame without direction. *7/187 8/188*

Now is imprisonment, afterwards fortune;
Finally casting off fetters and manacles. *9/189*

Notes

This is one of a number of Shou in which the text portrays two distinct kinds of imagery. In the first place, the name of the Shou, Release, indicates release from taxation and imprisonment. The other persistent image, less obvious from the translation, is the concept of shaking, enlivening, and excitation. The sun quickens nature; the wind shakes; the nobleman is excited, perhaps to anger. The phrase 'the high exalted nobleman' is possibly isolated, or may refer to the previous verse. This concept appears elsewhere in the work; see, for example, Shou 61.

Shou 22
Tsan 190-198
KE
A Pattern

格

Active flux;

Inner vigour can be the pattern, and so,
The multitudes seize upon it,
Likewise the closely-knit families. *1/190-3/192*

Quenching metal,
Melting stone,
Sending little,
Receiving abundantly. *4/193-6/195*

The outer wall is the eye;
Deformed is the flesh;
No dwelling there for the body, pulsating. *7/196-9/198*

格

Notes

The title of this Shou, KE, means a pattern in the sense of a model, grid, plan, or starting point, such as for example, the lines of latitude and longitude. 'Inner vigour' is such a model, seized on by the multitude, ever eager to follow the latest trends.

Metal and stone are two of the five elements of Chinese philosophy. Metals are not quenched, neither are stones melted: this is the incongruity picked up in the last verse of this text. The image is of a deformed animal, with two horns, one pointing up, the other down.

Shou 23
Tsan 199-207
I
Harm

Active flux.

Injury, scraping flesh from bones. *1/199*

Yin: not delivered from sickness. *2/200*

The element is consequently half changed. *3/201*

Tender baby daughter, baby son.
From the sign: three days.
No gruffness. *4/202-6/204*

Harm in age.
Advantage in being respectful;
Sickness a year. *7/205-9/207*

Notes

The character 'I' here has several readings, but the references to illness and injury in the text lead to the conclusion that 'harm' is the meaning intended.

The word 'changed' here is also 'I': the I of I Ching. I do not think that this is co-incidental; again I am inclined to believe that it is a either deliberate pun, or else that during the 'stream of consciousness' writing which produced the main, prognosicatory, body of the text, the image of Change (易) was formed.

Consisting almost entirely of sybilline phrases, the text needs no further comment.

Shou 24
Tsan 208-216
LO
Joy

樂

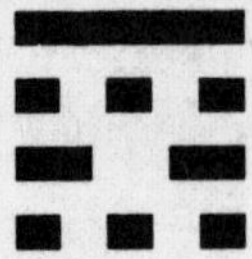

Yang begins to emerge.

Joy is spread out and folded up.
It is achieved by harmony and peace.
This element is the completion of happiness and joy.

Lost in happy thoughts,
Sincerity, sincerity. *1/208*

Extending
Not too distant. *2/209*

Joy is not . . .
The harmonious flux from Heaven.

Neither feasting nor elegance.
Sniffing, sobbing, dumbly gnawing;
These are the distinctive signs
of wailing at the door. *3/210*

Neither feasting nor elegance.
Propriety and joy waste away. *4/211*

Brush away the silken veils,
Cast off the bridal ornaments;
Perished is the spouse's heart. *5/212*

Great Joy, without speaking to the people's soul;
Birds of all kinds wheeling about in pleasure. *6/213*

Men shout for joy; demons shout for joy.
Heaven demands one year. 7/214

Self stand in awe;
No further transgression or mishap.

Joy from one extreme of the universe to the other. 8/215

But a day of grief:
The consequence: weeping and silently sobbing;
Sighs over the means of livelihood. 9/216

樂

Notes

Strangely enough, this extremely long text calls for very little comment. Note that it is one of the few Shou in the first forty texts which do not begin 'Yang Ch'i' but instead have a variant formula. Division of the text into Tsan, although there is no lack of text, has had to be made backwards from the last few verses, working towards the beginning. The latter verses are clear-cut, but the earlier verses seem to be lacking text.

The abrupt statement 'Joy is not' has no predicate; even the usually helpful gloss adds nothing to what appears to be a deliberately incomplete statement. The text is unpunctuated, but an incontrovertible gap appears before the commencement of the next verse.

Shou 25
Tsan 217-225
CHENG
Contention

爭

Active flux
Water overflowing:
Neither leaning to one side, nor leaning to the other.
This element is concerned with contention,
Litigation; all the honours in ritual ceremonial. *1/217*

Contention is not contention;
The Way is untrodden. *2/218*

Bright and glorious river;
Wasted thin. *3/219*

Contention is snarling, snarling. *4/220*

The Knight yields to his neighbours. *5/221*

Little profit;
Do not cut off the principal path
If it be dusk. *6/222*

Contention at the crossroads;
Advantage lacking direction. *7/223*

Ferociousness fills the mouth;
The arrow rests afterwards. *8/224*

Two tigers bare their teeth at each other;
Then they withdraw, knowing this perfection. *9/225*

爭

Notes

It is perhaps easy to see why this Shou should have been given the name 'Contention' since the tetragram clearly shows two opposing forces, one facing the other. It is not difficult to imagine the tetragram being the symbol for a mouth baring the teeth — the imagery of the latter verses — or even ferocious and angry words which led to strife and contention.

It is interesting to note that this text has an example of the 'A is not A' construction. There are two references to the Tao (The Way), which because of context, I have translated as 'Way' in the second verse, but as 'path' in the sixth.

The 'Crossroads' in the seventh verse may be a cross-reference to Shou 15, but see the commentary to that Shou. For the meaning of 'knight' see the commentary to Shou 20.

There is also a cross-reference in the commentary to Shou 58.

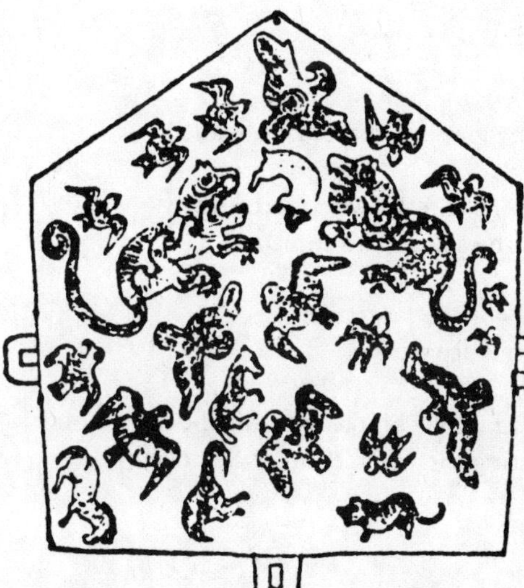

Shou 26
Tsan 226-234
WU
Scrutiny

Active flux.
Clearly scrutinizing the element thoroughly.

Conforming with the heart,
And also all material things, and their transactions. 1/226

Renewing the Self in fresh attire;
Bright is the Seal. 2/227

Do not grasp, neither hinder the heart
Lest the reasoning be destroyed. 3/228

To see the arrow rise itself;
Advantage in wings. 4/229

Friends. 5/230

Cover the load, the carriage is loaded. 6/231

The spider's threads when scrutinized
Are not the silkworm's threads. 7/232

Mourning is the fragrance
Lost in the departure. 8/233

Scrutinizing the completion of Self-destruction.
Obstructing the completion of Self-decline. 9/234

Notes

There are possible cross-references here to Shou 27 in the first verse, and to Shou 73 in the last verse. 'Friends' may be the end of the fourth verse, or the beginning of the next; reasons could be put forward for, or against, either interpretation.

Shou 27
Tsan 235-243
SHIH
Transactions

事

Active flux
Great glory and prosperity
The effulgence of the Sun rules this element;
Advantage is stretching, stretching out.

Every imitation is forced. *1/235*

Transactions lose transactions;
Attainment loses no transactions. *2/236*

Transactions are fixed at the pivot;
Neither consulted nor exhorted;
Their innate powers wither. *3/237*

Transactions between male and female —
Not betrothed, begetting children. *4/238 5/239*

The elder sage supports the orphaned child;
The tiny child knows the direction. *6/240*

Transactions between male and female —
Ten years; no admonishment. *7/241 8/242*

Reaching the ears: prosperous to stay,
Refusing to listen: prosperous to go. *9/243*

A ceremonial display of six divisions of troops.

. . . The Great Multitude are even more.
Darkness, all things beginning.
Fire enters the ears.
Tilling and ploughing ceases.
Shou 32

Shou 28
Tsan 244-252
KENG
Change

更

Active flux
Since flight alters the appearance of things,
The transformation of objects can be made by the intellect.

Time: 7.
Time: 9.
The carriage rolls along its way. *1/244 2/245*

Transmuting White
Into Black. *3/246*

The Boy, the Ox, the Horn, the Horse,
Are neither modern, nor ancient. *4/247 5/248*

Entering the water, a loaded cart;
Coming out of the water, a loaded barge.
Appropriate, in life, is Change. *6/249*

A team of four horses —
One horse is lame, is lame. *7/250 8/251*

Change drives a chariot
But it is hard going. *9/252*

更

Notes

One of the more interesting and exasperating texts, because of the mysterious reference to the numbers 7 and 9.*

First however, the name of the Shou itself. If the tetragram is compared with that of the previous Shou, No. 27, the transformation, or change, will be immediately apparent. The top line has changed from a single line into a broken one, while the other three tripled lines are all changed into unbroken lines.

*See introductory chapter, page 8.

This Shou is the first of the second main division of the 81 Shou, and is therefore not only the name of the next nine Shou collectively, but is also the head of the next 27 central Shou. At this point we would expect the 'active flux' to be gradually changing into the zero or neutral fluxes, just as one would presume that the final 27 Shou were all Yin. But as we shall see, this does not happen. Yang Hsiung indicates that the 'Yang' nature of the Shou lasts, gradually petering out, until the central Shou of all, No. 41, YING, Befitting. The text contains several synonyms for 'change' which have been here variously translated as alter, transmute, and so forth. Where 'Change' occurs in the text, this means that the original character was the Shou name, KENG.

The opening verse is extraordinary: it is a reference to the fact that things change their shape in flight. One immediately thinks of Einstein's theory of relativity, in particular the hypothesis of the FitzGerald-Lorentz contraction (first mooted in 1895) which suggests that a body moving through space at high velocity must contract.

The next line may suggest that either Yang Hsiung considered that it was possible to transform objects through thought alone, or else, more prosaicly, it was possible for the mind to imagine forms which did not already exist; as, for example, in the creation of a painting, or other imaginative work.

The second verse is tantalizing. An early commentary suggests that the number 7 refers to the system of 'changes' employed in calculating the tetragrams; but in fact the character 'Time' means a period of time; an event happening in seven days, months or perhaps years. The same explanation may be given for the next line, with regards to the number 9. The significance of this latter figure however is the division of the whole mechanics of the T'ai Hsüan into nines; furthermore, the number 9 figures very prominently in the mode of operation in consulting the I Ching by yarrow stalks. The numbers 7 and 9 have important significance with regards to the method of consulting the T'ai Hsüan; there are further references throughout the work to these numbers. See in particular, Shou 51, Rule.

The following line, sounding innocent enough in translation, bursts with all kinds of hidden meanings. The two characters which signify a carriage rolling along have, on their own, many other shades of meaning, which are not confined to the sense of revolving or turning, but can also mean pity and compassion. The two characters are also a palindrome of the expression 'to tune a lute'. Reading the text as poetry, one may not be concerned with these details, but where the text is used for divinatory purposes, these subtle tones could be important. But even more significantly (軫) Chen, the first of the characters for 'rolling carriage' is the name of the twenty-eighth constellation in the Chinese equivalent of our zodiac. Bearing in mind the possible references to constellations in verse four, it may not be a coincidence that this is the *twenty-eighth* Shou.

The 'black' of the next verse is not the usual word for black — that is, the charcoal black used for ink — but the colour of the black mud of the Shantung river. Shantung is well known for its silk, especially the black silk of the Tao priests' robes.

'The Boy, the Ox, the Horn, the Horse'. 'The Boy' is, of course, the name of the twelfth Shou, but we have here a list of possible references to constellations, including the Ox (Constellation 9), and the Horn (Constellation 1).

Concerning the team of four horses, it is perhaps interesting to recall an old Chinese saying 'A team of four horses cannot overtake the spoken word', or, as its English counterpart has it 'Once said, cannot be unsaid'. There is a reference to four horses in Shou 10. Also see reference to boats and carts in Shou 78 and 80.

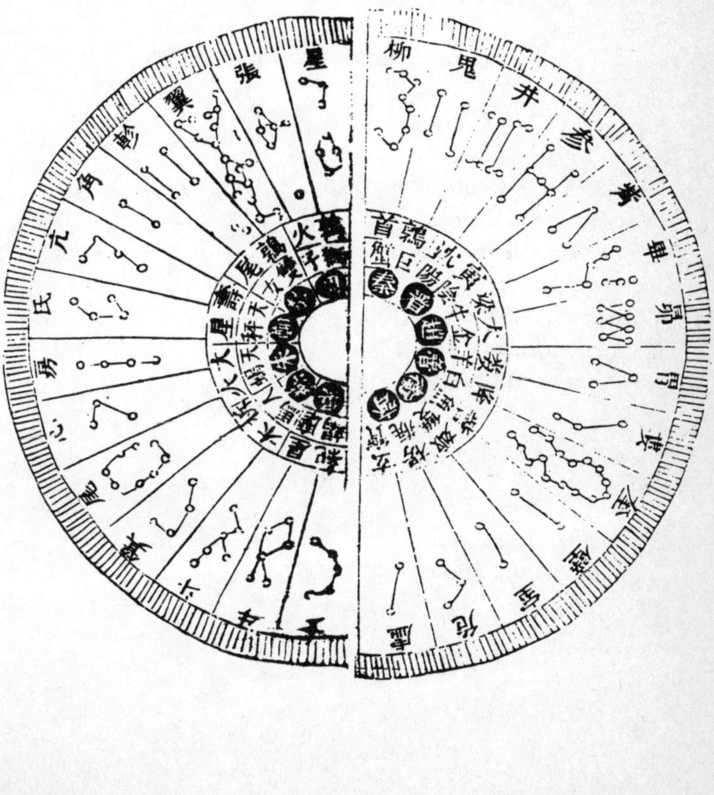

Shou 29
Tsan 253-261
TUAN
Severing

斷

Active flux.
A frontier inside, unyielding outside.

Exciting to action; still able,
Yet having (the right hand) severed,
Cut off completely. *1/253*

Severing the heart,
Obliterating the conscience. *2/254*

Thus the depths are marked out by the chalk-line
And the carpenter's square. *3/255*

Cut off are the deaf and those who cannot sense. *4/256*

Profit by curing foulness. *5/257*

The Great Belly cuts off its thighs,
Renounces the Knight,
And severs inferior people by moving. *6/258*

Cutting off is not cutting off;
Your enemy is not indulging;
So posterity will possess a halberd. *7/259*

7
Severing 2 *8/260*

My heart is like a peacock,
Full, and with a resplendent beauty. *9/261*

斷

Notes

The idea of 'severing' may be due to the appearance of the tetragram for this Shou, which shows two symmetrical arrangements of a strong line and broken line arranged back to back (or face to face, depending on ones viewpoint). Two different synonyms are used throughout: where the name of the Shou appears, this is translated as 'sever' but the synonym has been translated as 'cut off'. Both these characters appear in the last line of the second verse. One character is not clear: it may be 'right hand' or simply 'to possess'. Both make sense: 'Yu' (有) to possess, occurs two more times in this Shou, and it is not unusual for a character to be repeated several times during the course of a text, which would lead one to suppose that 'possess' was intended. However, 'Yu' (右) 'right hand' makes equal sense in the context.

'Anosmic', a medical term, is the only word in the English language which conveys the idea of one who cannot taste or smell, in the sense that 'deaf' and 'blind' indicate the loss of other senses.

The Arabic numerals 7 and 2 are here used to represent the Chinese quasi-numerals 庚 and 甲 which are respectively the seventh and second stems of the Chinese system of stems and branches. This is a numerical system by which the hours, days, months and years are measured. However, in addition to their numerical significance, these ancient characters also have more tangible meanings, although these are rarely used today. The Ming commentary suggests that by 7 is meant 'rites and ceremonies' and that 2 indicates 'moral uprightness'. It is curious that Yang Hsiung, having constructed a calendar built on a cycle of 9, should refer to the ancient Chinese calendar built on a joint cycle of ten and twelve. It may be relevant to observe that if 7 is severed from 9, the remainder is 2.

It is worth pointing out, with reference to the last verse, that 'K'ung' (meaning 'peacock') is the first syllable of the Chinese name of Confucius (K'ung Fu Tze).

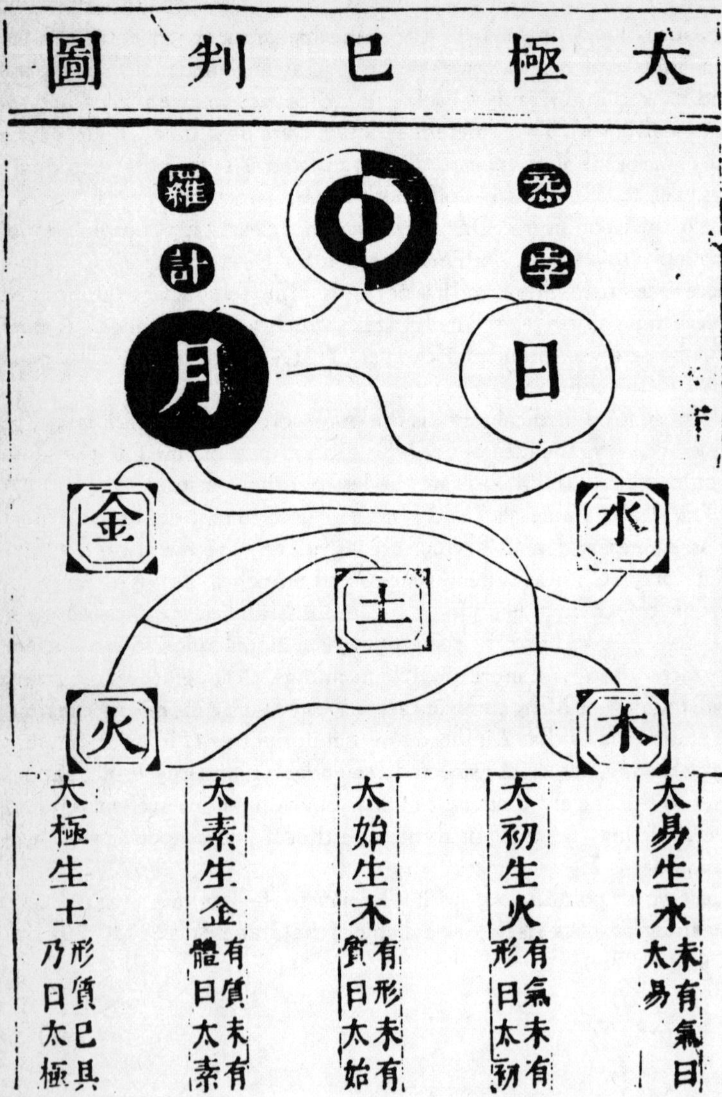

The T'ai Chi generating the Five Elements.

Shou 30
Tsan 262-270
I
Fortitude

毅

Active flux.
The direction of virtuous fortitude;
So therefore, in daring to act,
This element symbolizes such determination. 1/262

The bosom is stern; satisfaction is empty.
The Way to virtue is lost. 2/263

Fortitude in the heart and vitals.
Correctness. 3/264

Crowned by severity, fully satisfied,
The Knight does not have enough,
The inferior man has too much. 4/265

The Knight is not a utensil with only one use. 5/266

His speech carves; words are fortitude. 6/267

Fortitude is in the roof beams and pillars;
Profit is in the peaceful man's life. 7/268

The powerful ram shows fortitude;
The wood-pigeon is not a civet. 8/269

A boar's fortitude is in its teeth;
The officer, he goes hunting also. 9/270

Shou 31
Tsan 271-279
CHUANG
Pretence

裝

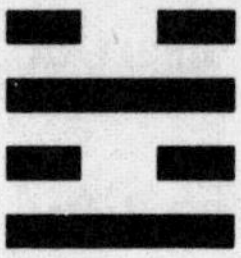

Active flux.
Even the great employ transactions;
Penetrating Yin, submission falls.

Pretence, and desire passes. *1/271 2/272*

Dark pretence.
One does not see its deeds. *3/273 4/274*

Dark pretence.
One does not see the heart;
Only the wrapping outside. *5/275*

The hawk-goose depends on the water;
The other winged creatures on the South Wind,
Riding in its bosom.

Departure is their determination,
And perhaps their happiness.
The starlings and the martins at dawn fly thick together
To the North; their melodious chirping and twittering
Making harmony, not stopping even to eat.

The swallows dart back and forth
Over the River Tzu,
Drinking and eating,
Prospering favourably,
Eating their fill.

The I Ching has six crossroads.
The Chou nine paths.
No boundaries to their deeds. *6/276*

The tradesman pretends to be stupid,
And thus may avoid being honoured. *7/277 8/278 9/279*

荘

Notes

Without any doubt, the most poetic of all the Shou texts, this little aviary of words demands a more literary treatment than is possible in an 'oracle' translation. The nature of the many birds portrayed in this text is unknown to me; even the Sung dynasty editor was puzzled by the 'hawk-goose' and suggested that it might be a roc or an albatross. Possibly nothing fabulous is intended, just a species of duck or goose which relied on water for safety and food. Several kinds of birds are described, and in each case the radical of the character suggests that the birds are large, or long-tailed. Contrast is made between those birds which 'ride in the bosom of the South Wind' and those which migrate northwards; between those which seem to spend their days twittering and making harmony, and the other birds which skim the river surface endlessly foraging for insects. No doubt the ornithologically-minded reader will be able to suggest which birds best fit these descriptions.

Then, with an abrupt change of direction, we are referred to the I Ching and the six lines of its hexagrams. The 'Chou', the name of the dynasty which preceeded the Han, is the name of the second Shou, but it also appears in the name of the I Ching as it is usually known to academics — the Chou I, or '(Book of) Changes of the Chou (Dynasty).' The number 9 may refer to the 'sixes' and 'nines' which are a feature of the I Ching method of divination, or it could be a reference to the recurrence of 9 in the T'ai Hsuan. (See also the commentaries to Shou 28.) It cannot be a coincidence that Shou 28 makes a reference to the numerical system of the I Ching, while the first line of this text (after the standard opening formula) refers to that Shou by name (Keng, Transactions.)

CHUANG, the title of this Shou, also has the meaning of 'to load up' which may have suggested the idea of packing up to move house — symbolized by the migration of birds.

Shou 32
Tsan 280-228
CHUNG
Multitude

衆

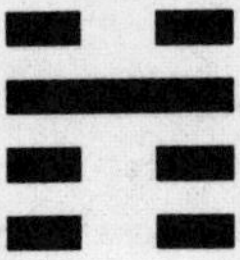

Active flux;
Expanding in the lofty vault
Nourishing the myriad things,
Proclaiming clearly
The great Multitude are even more.

Darkness, all things beginning.

Fire enters the ears;
Tilling and ploughing ceases.

The horse is guileless. *1/280*

A corpse is about to spread the fields. *2/281*

Without creativity,
Imitation is without avail. *3/282*

The guest doubts that he is a guest. *4/283*

The army doubts the advisability of chariots. *5/284*

Officers and men destroying children:
Internal violence — division.

The tiger's angry growl
Excites to action;
It is like an eagle,
But distinct from it.

The great all-thundering roar
Shakes and terrifies the ear.

Held together, using crimson silk,
Cradled in the arms. *6/285*

The flags and banners,
Woven from silken gauze,
On the halberds —
Moths, moths.

Imitation is conceiving. 7/286

Condolences in bereavement,
Grief dims the eyesight. 8/287

Declining and declining,
Seeing the sickness,
But not seeing the hearse. 9/288

衆

Notes

One of the longest texts in the T'ai Hsüan, and without doubt the most complex and baffling. The title of the Shou, Multitude, is picked up in the images of the army, tactical manoevres, battles and so on. While this may have little relevance to the individual, it must be remembered that in Yang Hsiung's times, oracles were often consulted on matters of State. These military verses are nevertheless interleaved with omens of a personal nature as well (e.g. 'condolences in bereavement'). Other verses may be incomplete; the usual pattern of an image, followed by a counterpoint, seems to be abandoned. Ch'en Jen Hsi has included a number of commentaries into the text; these may be his own, or they may be earlier glosses which he has copied. Here are the principle commentaries:

The horse is guilless. *To feed a horse with delicacies.*
A corpse is about to spread the fields. *Death of an elderly relative.*
A guest doubts that he is a guest. *Using force is not practicable.*
Held together using crimson silk. *Divisions within the heart.*
Imitation is conceiving. *The husband dies young; the wife is pregnant.*
To see the sickness, but not seeing the hearse. *Able to resist total submission.*

This Shou corresponds to the opening days of May, and the first few lines of text therefore refer to the ripening and flowering of crops. This may also account for the agricultural references in the text. Despite the idea of multitude being reflected in the images of the army, the proliferation of nature, and so on, it is remarkable that the title character appears only once in the text. (Compare with Shou 59, Assembly, where the title of the Shou does not appear at all in the text.) Equally remarkable is the imagery of the corpse and death, which is picked up in the glosses (see above). Unlike Shou 75, there is no 'pun' on the title character which might have explained this. It does however, contrast vividly with the image of 'pregnancy' suggested in lines 12 and 29. For a detailed explanation of the symbolism of 'pregnancy' in another context (which might equally well apply here) see Shou 64.

Shou 33
Tsan 289-297
MI
Intimacy

密

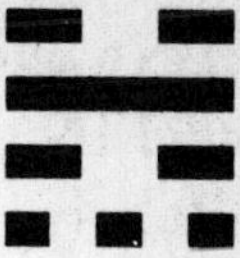

Active flux
Akin to Heaven.

The myriad things
Each one the refined beauty of the orchid. 1/289

United in intimacy;
Lacking questions. 2/290

Prying, but lacking the questions
Which are the gate to the great mysteries. 3/291

No intimacy, no comparison;
My heart is the young man's helper. 4/292

Intimacy in kinship;
Advantage in active people. 5/293

Intimacy within foul meat;
Three days, no perception of eating. 6/294

Intimacy of intimacy;
Does not cleave
The lady-guest from Heaven. 7/295

Polishing the teeth after gnawing. 8/296

Three harvests without a leader. 9/297

密

Notes
'Akin' in the first verse and 'kinship' in the fifth corresponds with the title of Shou 34.

MI also means 'close-meshed' as of nets, and is used in this sense in Shou 40.

Shou 34
Tsan 298-306
CH'IN
Relatives

親

Relatives revile their flesh and blood,
Their object; grinding teeth tightly locked. 1/298

Relatives revile their flesh and blood.
At the centre, the very heart is blocked. 2/299

Confidence in their flesh (and blood)
The purpose is wealth and kindred. 3/300

Wriggling grubs do not belong.
Wasps brook no insults from the naked. 4/301

Guests and relatives mindful of etiquette
Drink and eat quietly,
Not fussing, fussing. 5/302

Abundance is not abundance
Comparing men taking journeys. 6/303

Abudance upon abundance;
The knight is constant as the pole-star.
The exalted overreaches his position. 7/304

The granary is in compliance with transactions.
Dried meat in reserve; preserving dry food.
The trunk is a wrapper of excellence;
The Knight who goes travelling. 8/305

Dried foods for travelling:
Those are not my qualities. 9/306

親

Notes

The text has no introductory formula this time, but goes straight into the divinatory text without any reference to the nature of the Shou itself.

In the first two verses, the character construed here as 'flesh and blood' actually means 'skin'. This point is important bearing in mind the substance of later verses. In other senses however, the character means 'kindred'; 'grinding teeth tightly locked' means fierce opposition. In the third verse the term is this time 'flesh' rather than skin and bones, perhaps signifying confidence in wealth, rather than conflict in poverty in the first two verses.

The second half seems to compare two 'knights' (this word has already been explained in the commentary to Shou 20) one of whom makes provision for his journey, in the nature of dried meats, the other of whom refuses. Notice how the imagery of 'skin' and 'flesh' for relatives is picked up in the sense of dried meat. 'Trunk' can mean, as in English, either the trunk of a tree, or the trunk of the body — in this context is must be the latter. The comparison of the Emperor being like the pole-star, round whom all the Earthly world must turn, is also used by Shakespeare in *Julius Caesar*.

In the eighth verse, 'compliance' and 'transactions' are likely to be references to Shou 19 and 27 since these are so close together. The text, co-incidentally or not, abounds in allusions to other Shou, for example, Shou 4, a Barrier, (second verse) in the sense of a blockage, and Shou 78, Protection (sixth verse) in the sense of protecting those embarking on journeys. In this case the protection is in the form of foresight.

Shou 35
Tsan 307-315
LIEN
Accumulation

斂

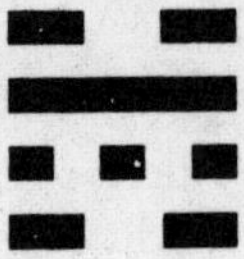

Active flux:
Great self-sufficiency on the outside;
Modicum of Yin:
A little accumulation on the inside.

A little accumulation: do not lend on interest.
Advantage in using a peaceful man
Remaining in the State. *1/307*

Ink accumulating:
Quibbling, wrangling,
Over that which illuminates. *2/308*

Seeing little, not making use;
Through my support afar off. *3/309*

Seeing little, not making use;
Waiting for my greatness. *4/310*

Abundance in retreat, moreover superabundance.
The silkworm cocoons are in the fields. *5/311*

Abundance in retreat, the silkworm cocoons
Do not snatch the timely opportunity. *6/312*

Weeping into silken veils;
Making the great one the chief;
While the inferior man does not show caution. *7/313*

The husband rides in a carriage
While the wife peels and scrapes.
Advantage lies with the King's aunt;
No advantage with the Duke's family. *8/314*

Accumulation improving; advantage.
Coercion to the limit results in calamity. *9/315*

歛

Notes

The character for Lien, (斂) the title of this Shou, is so similar to another, Han, (歛) that many dictionaries warn against confusing the two. It is not helpful, therefore that in the ancient text the character should have been written in such a manner as to appear to be a hybrid of the two very similar forms! However, inspection of the context reveals that the title of the Shou is likely to be Lien (accumulation) rather than Han (to beg for something coquettishly).

In the opening there verse is a reference to the greatness of Yang outside, and the minuteness of Yin on the inside; this is in direct contrast to Shou 9, which should be read in conjunction with the opening verse of this text. This contrast of smallness and greatness is taken up by the text at several points. The word which is used for 'aunt' also means to act under pressure, and this idea is reflected in the last verse in the warning against coercion.

The imagery of the silkworm cocoon is an allusion to purity.

Shou 36
Tsan 316-324
CHIANG (*CH'IANG*)
Boundary (*Violence*)

疆

Active flux.
Pure and simple, hard and enduring,
lasting, unyielding,
The myriad things.
There is nothing that has not CHIANG
The boundary, and a bridge.

Therefore hearing, therefore clearly,
To the left and to the right
The pounding drums, the pounding drums. *1/316 2/317*

Sufficient is my CHIANG
My frontier, and my bridge. *3/318 4/319*

In Heaven there is no boundary (*violence*). *5/320*

Metal unyielding, inside pliable;
Blood unstable; weakness in the fields. *6/321 7/322*

The boundary (*violence*) has a declining urge;
It weakens. *8/323 9/324*

疆

Notes

Chiang is a boundary between fields; the graph for a field appears in the character itself. The 'pounding of drums' is a visual pun, the character (扌畺) having a superficial resemblance to that for Boundaries. Note the connecting link with the previous Shou is the word 'pure' based on the silkworm cocoon.

The characters for Chiang (疆) boundary and Ch'iang (彊) violence, are sometimes interchanged. Alternative readings are offered where the context seems to suggest it.

Therefore hearing, Therefore clearly,
To the left and to the right,
The pounding drums, the pounding drums.
Shou 36

太玄準易卦名圖

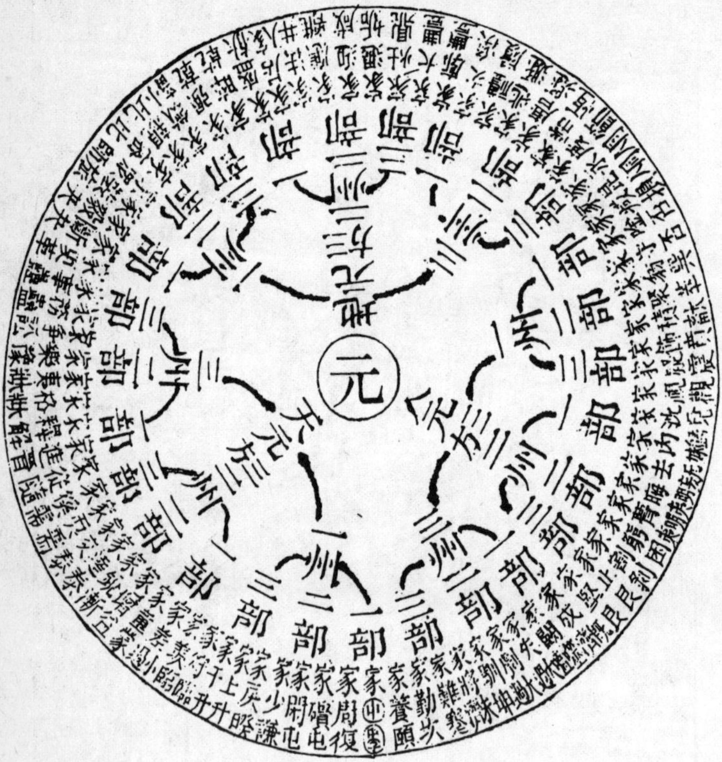

The Year divided into 81 Shou. From a Sung dynasty edition of the T'ai Hsüan Ching.

Shou 37
Tsan 325-333
TSUI
A Year

晬

Active flux.
Now equally balanced,
The year at its brightest,
This element has the greatest light.
It protects the divisions of the Sun's
Brightness and activity.

The Year is lucid within —
As water cleared of weeds.

There is no contradiction;
The cycle of the year returns to the centre.

The eye looks upwards towards the Heavens;
The ear listens to the abyss below.

The Great Year receives;
Error changes.

晬

Notes

This Shou is the beginning of the fifth *T'ien*, and corresponds to the end of June and the beginning of July, thus incorporating the Summer Solstice, which corresponds to Tsan 365 in Shou 41. Its appearance here is not contradictory, if one remembers that the opening Shou of each *T'ien* covers the next nine Shou inclusive. (Refer to the calendar tables, where this point will be made clear.) As all of this text, apart from the fourth verse, is of a philosophical nature, it has not been divided into Tsan. For divinatory purposes, refer to the Lo Shu; see the remark in 'The Tsan Texts' page 55.

Shou 38
Tsan 334-342
SHENG
Abundance

盛

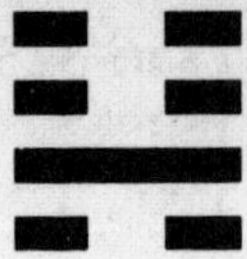

Active flux.
Surpassing abundance; bottled up;
This element shows genuineness and certainty;
Entirely full, symbolizing ideas. *1/334*

SHENG is not dark and abstruse;
It is an arrow pointing to correct action. *2/335*

Deeds are not dependent
On having great possessions. *3/336*

Deeds are not dependent
On being in concordance with the secret in the bosom. *4/337*

Nurturing advantages in the bosom of the full-hearted:
There is no advantage for the Duke. *5/338*

Small abundance:
Officers of state and civil servants
Wait at the great man's door. *6/339*

Whosoever, when happiness is full, mentions calamity,
Should resign, should resign. *7/340*

Producing fire, producing cold,
The fountain is reached. *8/341*

Ladling from that full and sparkling fountain;
Afterwards pouring is out. *9/342*

盛

Notes
'The pounding of the drum' relates to Shou 36.
'Public' can be read for 'Duke' in the fifth verse.

Shou 39
Tsan 343-351
CHÜ
A Dwelling

居

Active direction.
Stability.

A skin:
Gloriously resplendent,
Because of this element's outer fortifications.
The myriad things are united under the law.

The family lacks pots;
The wife inherits her aunt's;
Perhaps they are dirty,
Perhaps they are clean. *1/343-3/345*

The aged father changes his clothes;
The carriage is too small.
The woman lifts the pots.
Advantage is examining the family. *4/346-6/348*

Turning the table over;
A couple are compared.
Their family is not stable. *7/349-9/351*

居

Notes
Although the title of this Shou does not appear in the text, the imagery used is perfectly relevant, all being concerned with family and domestic matters. The least mystical of the texts, it can be compared with Shou 44, the Stove.

Shou 40
Tsan 352-360
FA
Law

法

Active flux

The most exalted region is the Law.
This is the element which respects ink.

There is nothing that is not washed clean
By the Rule.

A silken thread, drawn, drawn out. *1/352*

The sacrificial vessels neglect the belly. *2/353*

The well is vast and deep,
There is death through not getting food. *3/354*

The sacrificial vessels neglect the belly;
They are not learning the direction. *4/355*

A finely-meshed net is dredging the abyss;
There is no advantage in overlapping. *5/356*

A finely-meshed net dredges the abyss;
Vexations laws are laid out. *6/357*

The well lacks the trunk.
The tree is upright. *7/358*

Gone is the rivulet,
Gone is the valley. *8/359*

The end is in error. *9/360*

法

Notes

The substance of this text compares Heaven's immutable laws with earthly government, bad or evil. Food may be used for official sacrfices while people starve. There are several cross-correspondences between this Shou and others. More importantly are: the finely-meshed net, which is an alternative reading of MI, (Shou 33), the 'ink' in Shou 38; and the 'Well'. The latter is not only one of the names of the hexagrams of the I Ching, but also one of the constellations mentioned in Shou 28. In addition, the reference to the long-drawn silken rope recalls the broken well-rope in the commentaries to the 'Well' in the I Ching. (This verse may also be read 'Wells, lakes, and oceans . . .'). Elsewhere, there is a gloss to the effect that 'direction' is an oblique reference to the Tao, the Way.

Shou 41
Tsan 361-369
YING
Befitting

應

The first half of the calendar has been displayed;
The second half is regulated in harmony with it;
One line proceeds vertically, one line proceeds horizontally;
Heaven's laws are woven together, enmeshed, enmeshed.

The Dragon flies up to Heaven;
The Divination strides over the overlaps.

Blazing fire reaches down from Heaven;
Icicles sprout from the Earth.

The Chief Brightness reaches its limits;
The knight, by what is befitting, becomes great.

應

Notes

This is the central Shou of the entire 81; consequently we would not expect to find the formula 'Yang Ch'i' anymore. The Dragon, associated with floods, is one of the four quarters of the sky; it is referred to elsewhere in the T'ai Hsüan, (See, for example, Shou 1 verse 4).

The change from 'Active' to 'Recessive' forces is indicated by the topsy-turvy reversal of the fire and ice. The 'Chief Brightness' refers to the Summer Solstice, the sun's maximum brightness occuring on the day of Tsan 365, the central day of the year.

The meaning of the second half of the first verse is probably a reference to the appearance of the tetragram itself, or it could allude to the square, 9×9, of the 81 Shou arranged in rows, vertically and horizontally (See page 6). This Shou is too brief to be divided into Tsan. See the remarks on page 55.

Shou 42
Tsan 370-378
YING
Greeting

迎

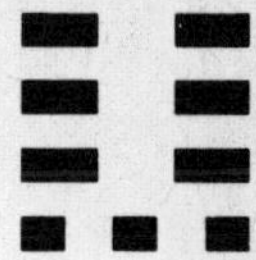

Recessive flux.
The completed form of the first half of the elements is united, flows against the current, and meets with this element in greeting.

The Scaly Dragon lies beneath the water
In the abyss. *1/370*

Crossing the water, at the third hour
The transformation of man is completed. *2/371*

Through Yin's words
One hundred clans are in harmony. *3/372*

The scaly dragon, lying hidden under water
Transform the Centre;
The essential quality is sincerity. *4/373*

The quintessential quality comes and goes;
The weird preferences of the intelligence and
consciousness. *5/374 6/375*

The Secret and the Yellow greet each other;
Their ideas affecting each other mutually. *7/376 8/377*

To see blood enter the door;
Cherishing the greeting in the Central Chambers. *9/378*

迎

Notes
The first Shou to begin with 'Recessive flux' formula; this formula is however omitted from most of the Shou in the second half.

The *Ssu*.

The *Hsi*.

Shou 43
Tsan 379-387
YU
Meeting

遇

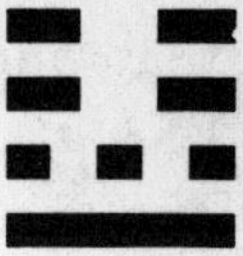

Gloomy meeting with the spirit;
Contemplation lines like the veins in jade. *1/379-3/381*

Rushing, rushing to the meeting with the child.
The son has no likeness. *4/382 5/383*

Neither departing, nor coming,
Obtaining from the sage woman the divination. *6/384-8/386*

Two rhinoceros fight;
one is lamed,
Not vanquished or killed. *9/387*

遇

Notes

Later editions of the text add the standard formula to this and other Shou which do not begin Yin Ch'i.

The 'rhinoceros' of the last verse is (probably) a mythical animal, described as having one horn, but of bovine rather than equine appearance, hence, not the unicorn of Western myth. It is also mentioned in Shou 6, and illustrated opposite. Bronze vessels in the shape of this beast were used in ancient ceremonies, and another kind of vessel of this appearance was used to collect the token counters at archery contests. (See also Shou 44 and 45.)

Shou 44
Tsan 388-396
TSAO
The Stove

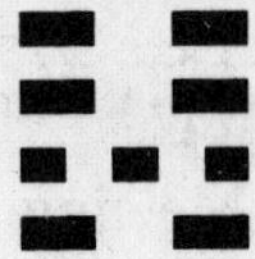

Recessive, although fertilizing and flowing;
The active is similarly taking hold, and in harmony.

The Stove lacks provisions;
Entreaties from a neighbour. *1/388*

The Yellow Ting is hollow;
Its centre and its border;
Neither food nor drink;
Trusting, lacking harm. *2/389 3/390*

The stove lacks fuel;
Its edges are made of gold. *4/391*

The cauldron has provisions; its food
Reaches out its savour strongly. *5/392*

The cauldron has provisions;
Its food is timely.
I reach up with both hands respectfully to receive it. *6/393*

The Ting:
The great are feasting,
Neither solemnly nor sedately. *7/394*

Ox suet:
The prime fat was not cleansed.
The Fou is boiled;
The result: vomiting black poison;
Then sickness is attained. *8/395 9/396*

竈

Notes

As one would expect in the central core of the 81 Shou, here the combining of the active and recessive forces is described. The imagery in the first half of the text alludes to want: the golden sacrificial vessels have no food in them. The second half of the text suggests that although there are provisions enough to make a feast, the proper rites and ceremonies have been neglected; consequently, such elementary hygiene precautions as cleaning the fat having been disregarded, the result is sickness, and vomiting 'black meat'.' (See also Shou 47.)

'Ting' and 'Fou' (see also Shou 43 and 45) are types of ceremonial cooking pots of solemn ritual significance. Many Chinese bronzes, of exquisite workmanship, have survived because these venerated articles, associated with clan ancestors, were included among tomb burial objects. Even the very casting of these bronzes was attended with great ceremonial, and they frequently had accurately dated dedicatory inscriptions.

In imagery, this Shou is the equivalent of the fiftieth hexagram of the I Ching, Ting, the cauldron. There is, however, an interesting detail concerning this word. Karlgren, in 'Grammata serica recensa' points out that Ting (鼎) was originally a loan for Chen (貞) the fourth character of the opening formula of the I Ching, translated in some editions as 'upright' but also meaning to inquire by divination, and is the technical term for the lower half of the diagrams of the I Ching. On ancient bone inscriptions, the graph for cauldron was () and the pronunciation Tieng was similar to the sound Cheng, the ancient form of Chen (to inquire by divination, etc.) Later, to distinguish these two characters, the mark Po (卜) was added to Cheng, thus (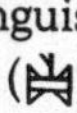), (this graph meaning to inquire by means of tortoise carapace or scapula, the character being a representation of the cracks on the carapace or bone) so that by the time these two words had acquired distinctive pronunciations, they had also lost any similarity of appearance. It may well be that the fiftieth hexagram of the I Ching was not Ting, cauldron, but Chen, an altogether more abstract concept.

The character translated here as 'poison' is one which was supposed to be obtained from the wings of a certain black bird: it was sufficient just to dip the feathers of the bird into wine in order to poison it.

Shou 45
Tsan 397-405
TA
Great

大

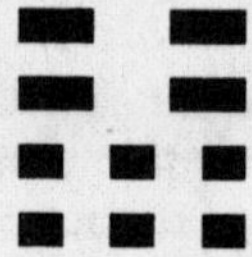

The Recessive force, empty, stays in the Active force,
Entangled; it is outside the element,
But together with it, like a pan and its lid.

The abyss, the lake, the sea:
Wrapped round without direction.

Great is the scheme;
The body's Self being burnished. *1/397*

Great is not Great;
By means of advantage, greatness is achieved. *2/398*

Great is the door into the wilderness
Not being ploughed.
The cries of birds in the emptiness. *3/399*

Great is the door into the wilderness
The substance of recognition: fame will come. *4/400*

Great losses — small.
Greater losses — too small. *5/401*

Great extravagance distorts the Self
By scraping away the corners.
Perhaps there is benefit at the time of the evening meal. *6/402*

Great extravagance distorts the Self
By scraping away ones own abilities.
It must be avoided. *7/403*

The Li: *8/404*

The wall is precipitous;
The foundations are not beaten down hard.
In three years it falls in ruins. *9/405*

大

Notes

It is remarkable how the imagery suddenly changes in the last verse. There are no references to earlier verses, as is usually the case. Even the opening character, Li, a sacrificial vessel (see Shou 44) stands on its own like a title, as if an altogether different Shou were intended here — the remains, perhaps, of a forgotten symbol. There is no relevance at all to the wall built on shaky foundations.

What appears to be a feature of the style of the writing of the T'ai Hsüan is that sometimes the shape of a character seems to suggest, consciously or unconsciously, the basis of a new image, as if one character were being transmuted into another. It is as if a word such as 'peat' should stimulate the imagination to produce — not a rhyming word, like 'heat', but a similar word in appearance, like 'pear'. There is no tangible evidence on which one can lay a finger, as one can with, for example, the formula 'A is not A' which occurs several times throughout the work as a whole. Nevertheless, the notion is one which might give a clue into Yang Hsiung's creative thought processes. In this text, the reference point is the word 'scraping' (削) which seems to have suggested the idea of 'precipice' (峭). Karlgren (op. cit. Shou 44) has pointed out that although in modern Chinese these two words have entirely different pronunciations, they would have had a similar sound in archaic Chinese (a millenium before Yang Hsiung, however) 'scraping' being *s'iog* 'precipice' *ts'iog*.

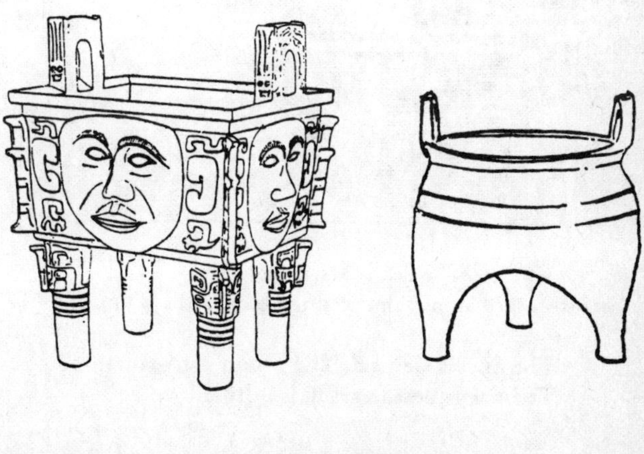

Ting (see pp 135, 149) and Li.

The Pearl-Geared Jade Rail
An ancient astronomical instrument of the time of the Shun, 2255-2205 BC.

The Sun is Central, The Moon surpassing;
The brightness, fearful, is eclipsed.
Shou 67

Shou 46
Tsan 406-414
K'UO
Extending

廓

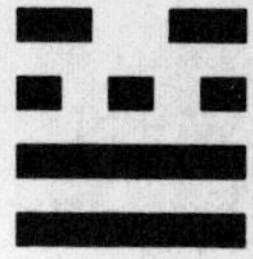

Metal trunks, and jade posts,
Extending the city walls. *1/406*

Extending is without a son,
The house of stone is without a housewife. *2/407*

Heaven's gates are flung wide open:
The vast hall and the staircase;
Consider whether life has been in error. *3/408*

Heaven's gates are flung wide open.
Virtue is unable to enter the lake palace. *4/409*

Outside is great expansion;
At the centre, loss. *5/410*

The knight reaches the wilderness;
The humble person enters his house. *6/411*

Extending outside into emptiness;
Inside is advantage.
Drums and gongs. *7/412*

Extending outside into emptiness;
Inside however, one has possessions.
The divination is audible. *8/413*

The central pillar of the Extending
Is manifested high overhead.

Three years without a boy. *9/414*

廓

Notes:

The final characters of the third and ninth verses respectively are the names of the eleventh and twelfth Shou, Ch'a (差) and T'ung (童). See the notes to Shou 64.

Shou 47
Tsan 415-423
WEN
Literature

文

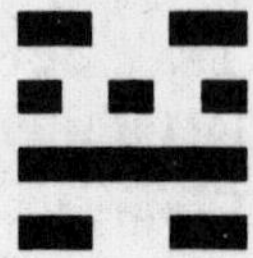

Yin craves the assistance of Yang
In the creation of literature.
Literature craves publication.
Publication craves literature.

The myriad things
Are thus marked out and are blazed abroad.

The three-yearly sacrifice will be auspicious
If there is no negligence; 1/415

What of the silken threads
To wrap round the jade ornaments? 2/416

Great literature unadorned
Is like the stump of a severed foot. 3/417

The vast amount of literature lacks pattern;
Throw restraint into the river. 4/418

The vast amount of literature lacks pattern
And restrains the flow of ideas as they come and go. 5/419

The collared pheasant does not prosper
But the tern is faithful and loyal. 6/420

The collared pheasant does not prosper;
The raven nourishes gloom. 7/421

Engraving quibbles on flimsy paper for publication;
Lacking time for literature;
Consequence: rebellion. 8/422

The limits of literature are means of enmeshed, enmeshed.
Change by the sacerdotal vestments. 9/423

文

Notes

The second character of this text is the hybrid character which might be Lien, Accumulation (Shou 35) or to crave, Han. Here it has been translated as 'crave'.

Ancient texts refer to the wrapping of silken threads round ceremonial objects during the rites; this recalls the Ancient Egyptian practice of swathing the images with lengths of linen. One of the ceremonial objects, the jade Tsung, had little notches carved into its flanges which may well have been to wrap the threads round.

The character for 'close-meshed' repeated at the end of the end of the penultimate line is MI, Shou 33.

The sacerdotal vestments referred to in the last verse were black robes embroidered with stripes or axes.

This text is interesting in that it reflects Yang Hsiung's ideas on literary style, which he describes in another work. He believed that ideas should be allowed to flow spontaneously, and that constraints of style were to be avoided.

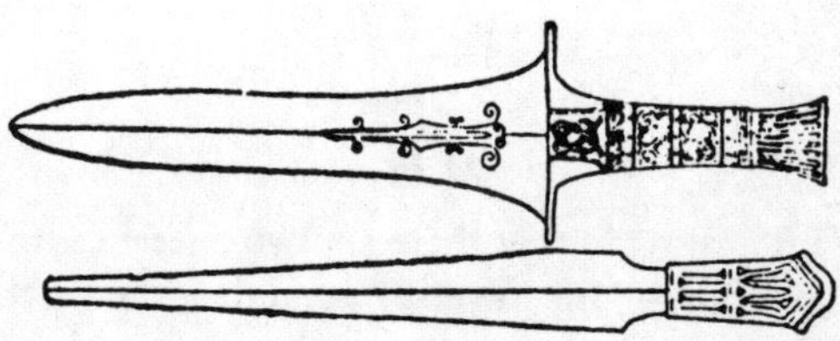

Shou 48
Tsan 424-432
LI
Propriety

禮

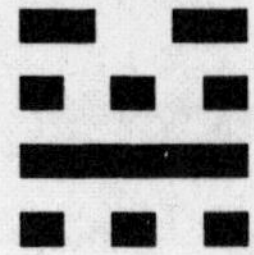

A shoe for a foot with six toes:
Descendants worship their ancestors. *1/424*

A shoe for a foot with six toes:
Withdrawal from their relatives. *2/425 3/426*

The eye is solemn, solemn;
The foot reverential, reverential.
So one threads through the brambles. *4/427 5/428*

The lines of the I Ching diagrams
Are interpreted by their appearance;
Contemplation without completion. *6/429*

Fish scales overlapping: error
But great benefits;
Those employed by the Supreme One rise to
  Heaven. *7/430 8/431*

Advantages lacking this Shou:
How may one use the 9? *9/432*

禮

Notes

This Shou is interesting in that there are two references to the I Ching method of divination — one in verse 4, and the other in the last verse. The number 9 has an important role in the reading of the lines in the I Ching, as well as the T'ai Hsüan.

The curious opening verse is a very complex word game. The name of the Shou, LI, meaning propriety, is a homonym of Li (履) ceremonial conduct. But this word also means a shoe, while 'a foot with six toes' also means to stand on tiptoe, or to creep — hence the reverential steps in the third verse. The image of 'threading' in that verse is conveyed by a string of cash — coins threaded on a cord.

Shou 49
Tsan 433-441
T'AO
Escape

逃

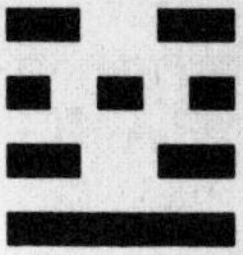

Escaping water's injury;
Obliterating the wound's scars. 1/433

Escaping water's injury;
The scars are not the wounds. 2/434

The heart is overawed, overawed;
The foot wears a golden slipper.
There is no ambition;
The ditch becomes a raging torrent. 3/435

Wrangles and divisions; 4/436

Flogging a horse;
Tyranny and cruelty at the door;
It is better to escape.

See the birds, kicking in the thicket;
Entering into the abyss, attacking. 5/437

More fields not roped off;
Waste; I doubt its merit. 6/438

Roped up;
Later, therefore, they can fly. 7/439

Roped up; almost
Hidden; do not step high. 8/440

The neck is lengthened by arrow and string;
Tied, the ends of the marking cords. 9/441

(See the notes to Shou 50.)

Shou 50
Tsan 442-450
T'ANG
The Dodder-plant

唐

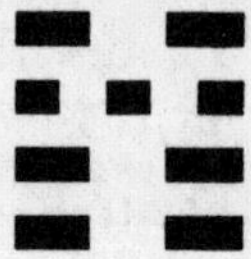

The Dodder-plant; 1/442

A long rope is not auspicious. 2/443

There lacks the dragon-shaped gem,
And the other jade ornaments. 3/444

The running deer longs to be a mouse;
It succeeds — it is not restrained. 4/445-6/447

Bright pearls,
Playing on lutes
Flying fingers
Such achievement — not to be repeated. 7/448-9/450

唐

Notes

Just as the previous Shou picked up the image of the foot in the Shou before it, so the rope, as it were, dangles from the last Shou to this. The idea of 'escaping' is transferred to the deer, but whereas in 'Escape' there were the restraints of rope mentioned in almost every verse, in this short text the deer has escaped. A totally different picture is then presented; 'bright pearls (that is, eyes or teeth flashing) and fingers flying over lute strings — producing elation it would not be thought possible to repeat. What then, has this to do with the dodder-plant? Apparently, nothing at all. The dodder was regarded as a sacred plant, in the same way that the mistletoe was by the Celtic priesthood — on account of the fact that it was a parasitic plant, without roots. To ward off any evil spell in gathering it, a young boy was sent to collect it (the Boy of Shou 12, and the I Ching hexagram 4, where it is called Meng). As he gathered it, he would repeat the charm 'It is not I who comes to collect the dodder, it is (so-andso)', that is, in fact, the words of the I Ching text to the fourth hexagram. T'ANG has many other meanings besides 'dodder-plant'. It was also the name of the Emperor Yao, and was thus associated with the glories of a past Golden Age. It also referred to the path which led from a temple's entrance-gate to the main hall.

Shou 51
Tsan 451-459
CH'ANG
Rule

常

Crowned by a spirit in black.
Ceremony is the medium whereby
The Genius communicates through the divining board.

By means of one image
Ten thousand ends are not concluded. *1/451*

The Sun's principles are the virtues.
Three years, there is no food. *2/452 3/453*

Attaining 7
Also 9. *4/454 5/455*

The timid yield to the unyielding
unable to rule; *6/456*

Rule: sickness is not sickness;
Ill omens completing, do not explain it. *7/757 8/458*

Sickness is sickness;
It is cured by the wizard,
Not the doctor. *9/459*

常

Notes

The divining board was used to communicate with the spirits, not in the manner of the planchette, but in some other way which we can only conjecture. Several representations of it — indeed actual examples — have been found in Han dynasty (contemporary with the T'ai Hsüan) tombs. Note that the word 'ceremony' in the second line is the same as that for 'shoe' in Shou 48. Again there is reference to 7 and 9 (see Shou 28). 'Wizard' or shaman, can be taken to mean a non-conventional healer (also see Shou 75).

Shou 52
Tsan 460-468
TU
A Degree

度

Recessive flux
The Sun is fierce;
Active flux,
The Sun is resting.
Fiercely, fiercely,
Resting, resting;
Each is allotted its proper degree.

Boards are not boards;
Torn off from buildings. *1/460*

The Great Degree searches, searches;
In the sky is an omen;
A sign of importance — it is grass. *2/461 3/462*

Not a degree of the compasses;
Demons restrain the heir. *4/463 5/464*

Not a degree of the compasses;
Clearly examining the laughter. *6/465*

The stone is red; do not hold it;
The economy of the scholar is a necessity *7/466 8/467*

Amassing error; lending money on interest;
After ten years there is still no return. *9/468*

度

Notes
The 'boards' in the second verse are used to cover, and protect, a well-mouth.

Shou 53
Tsan 469-477
YUNG
Eternity

永

By Yin the military are killed;
By Yang the literary learn: 1/469

The Way which lasts for ever. 2/470

Neither sorrowful, nor lively,
For ever last those Heavenly precepts. 3/471

Neither sorrowful, nor lively,
Eternity is the Way of the ancestors. 4/472

In the bosom there is sorrow and joy;
Eternity loses the good and bad omens. 5/473

The Master has precedence,
No precedence for the guest of honour;
Eternity errs in life. 6/474

Great Eternity; therein good fortune;
Turning away from the empty audience chamber. 7/475

Entering into the perfect world. 8/476

The ancient trees live eternally and upright,
By being swathed in their places where they are at fault. 9/477

永

Notes

The military and literary professions were regarded as opposites, equivalent to Yang and Yin respectively; the allusion would have been familiar to Yang Hsiung's readers.

Shou 54
Tsan 478-486
K'UN
Posterity

昆

Yin protects married couples;
Yang guards their posterity;
Their posterity is the Way;
That is in charge of both. 1/478

Posterity is in blackness;
It is not like whiteness. 2/479

Posterity is in blackness;
It is not like the speech of man. 3/480

White and black are fragrant, fragrant. 4/481

Three kinds of creature; one flesh; all similarly tailed. 5/482

Birds prefer their nests to be in dense thickets;
Man lodges his fate in public. 6/483

Birds prefering their nests in public
Lack desires. 7/484

The Marten errs, treading cautiously.
The multitude of tailed creatures destroys jade. 8/485

Hiding, prejudiced, not repeating these words.
Clear skies; rain not sparing. 9/486

昆

Notes

The word 'multitude' = Shou 32.

This is the final Shou of the 'central' block, representing the zero forces.

The ringed pheasant, calling its particular note, approaches the ceremonial Ting, while one of the court musicians indicates the appropriate chime. This was regarded as a particularly felicitous omen.

See Shou 63

Shou 55
Tsan 487-495
CHIEN
Diminishing

減

The heart diminishes,
The Self at the Centre.
By its form in the body.

Diminishing the ceremonies. 1/487

Advantage in using light on the stairs.
Diminishing the artemisia. 2/488

Disparaging the social order. 3/489 4/490

The obscure is explained:
Storing up; no diminishing,
Not granting the Stone. 5/491 6/492

The appearance of deep water, running deep, 7/493 8/494

Diminishing from life's foundations. 9/495

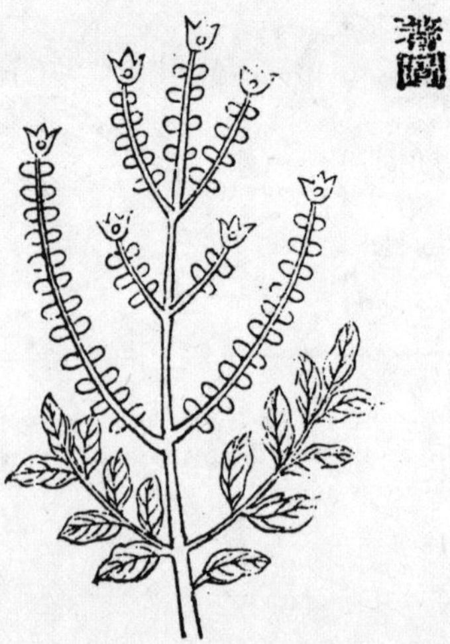

滅

Notes

The artemisia, or mugwort, was an important medicinal herb. Its dried leaves and stems were ground into a powder and burnt, the burning punk being applied to certain parts of the body. This ancient skill, known as 'moxibustion' on account of the fact that the mugwort punk was called moxa, is of course allied to acupuncture. The artemisia is a relative of the yarrow, whose stalks were used in divination, and it is worth noting that the character for artemisia (艾) consists of the 'flower' radical (艹) together with the Yao character (乂), meaning one of the lines of the diagrams of the I Ching. The ancient commentary concludes that this Tsan indicates recovery from illness.

'Light on the stairs' is a prosaic translation; it probably means 'glory of increasing rank' in view of the reference to the 'social order'.

This is the first Shou of the final third, corresponding to the 7th, 8th, and 9th T'ien, the whole section representing 'Earth'.

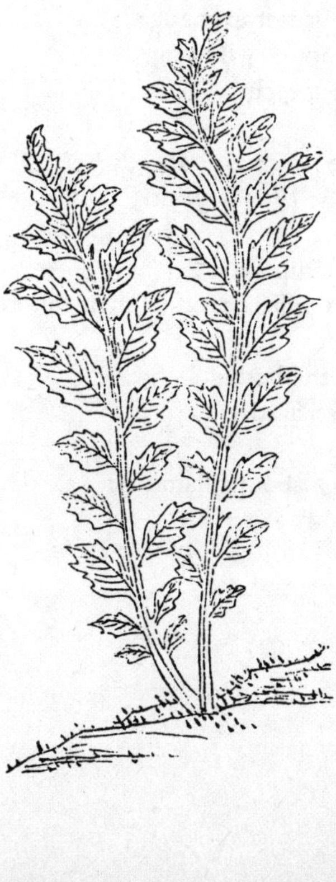

艾圖

Shou 56
Tsan 496-504
YIN
Humming

唫

Yin is not transforming,
Yang is not bestowing;
The myriad things all hum.

Humming is not the son,
The Elders, the husband and wife dwelling together. 1/496

Humming is in the blood;
Property is dry bones. 2/497

Humming is in the blood;
Burning away the Self's fattiness. 3/498

The appearance is not exchanged;
The mouth clamours, gabbling;
Humming lacks speech. 4/499

The appearance is not exchanged;
For mankind, the Way is trifling. 5/500

Not central; not supervised;
Corrupt, grubby officials, off to their miseries. 6/501 7/502

Humming is in the body;
Yellow flesh destroyed. 8/503

Humming brings about calamities;
Prayers with an ox fattened. 9/504

唫

Notes

Although translated here as 'humming' Yin can also mean 'chanting'. In view of the reference to ritual sacrifice in the last verse, it is probably best to consider this alternative meaning; indeed, it is possible that most of the verses in this mystic text refer to sacrifice. The last verse is actually a suggestion that to avert calamaties, an ox should be sacrificed with the appropriate prayers.

Note the features of this text: it begins Yin, which may well be another pun (see Shou 19, Ts'ung). Again, there seem to be visual similarities between characters, as if one character has suggested a particular train of thought.

Further remarks on this are in the commentary to Shou 45.

'Exchanged' in the fifth and sixth verses is the name of Shou 16. See the notes on the life of Yang Hsiung, page 24, for a remark about his speech impediment.

Shou 57
Tsan 505-513
SHOU
Protection

守

Yin protects the window;
Yang protects the door.
The elements do not oppose each other.

Closing off friends with a lattice window.
Protection is the chief possession. *1/505-3/507*

Deluding the Self's protection.
Unlike a single possession. *4/508*

A carriage and a bench: the cross-bar of a carriage;
A jade tablet and a house-wall: dust. *5/509*

A mortar lacks a pestle;
Hands lift it up. *6/510*

Heaven's Yin is not rain;
The White Sun destroys it. *7/511*

Taking tea together;
There is protection of speech;
By the black stove:
This Shou is not perilous. *8/512*

Taking tea together;
There is protection:
Weighing things over,
Pondering over what is new. *9/513*

守

Notes
The jade tablet was a symbol of rank and authority; a house a symbol of wealth.

Note that this diagram is the reverse of that of Shou 25 q.v.

Shou 58
Tsan 514-522
HSI
Re-uniting

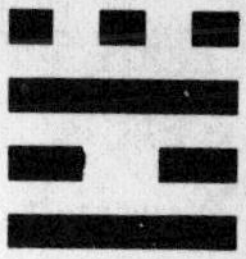

Going towards the highway while it is still dark.
Re-uniting in ambition. 1/514

Although slight desires,
Brushing them aside;
Heaven has not set the appointed time. 2/515

Re-uniting darkness with the centre;
The body is an auspicious omen. 3/516

Re-uniting with food:
Lapping, lapping.
Advantage, as if posturing. 4/517

Re-uniting their wings;
Advantage in employment; lifting up. 5/518 6/519

Re-uniting their divisions. 7/520

Spinning the golden threads. 8/521

Yellow is the heart.
The wild-geese shelter;
Re-uniting in Heaven. 9/522

Notes

Yellow is the Imperial colour; also the colour of Earth. Compare the opening line with Shou 25, sixth verse.

Shou 59
Tsan 523-531
CHÜ
Assembly

聚

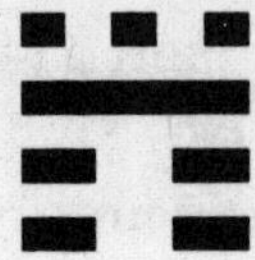

Demons and spirits;
Lacking genii. *1/523*

Ancestors in memorial year:
Demons at the gate. *2/524 3/525*

Pulling the whole;
Omens in thickets are fortunate. *4/526*

Grasping the jade tablet:
A promise to the left flank. *5/527*

The Ting is full of blood and foul water-weeds. *6/528*

Nine ancestors show goodness;
Posterity has confidence. *7/529 8/530*

Owls and pigeons sit in the woods;
A parliament of the other multitudes of life. *9/531*

聚

Notes

For a reference to the jade-tablet, see Shou 57; for Ting, see Shou 44.

It is difficult to translate the various concept of spirits demi-gods, and other supernatural creatures. I have translated as 'demons' the disembodied spirits which had no resting place, and are denied eternal bliss; they are sometimes translated as 'ghosts'.

By 'spirits' are meant the demi-gods, the possible equivalent of dryads and the like. 'Genii' are celestial intelligences. These latter two words are sometimes used to indicate the human spirit and intelligence. They are mentioned several times throughout the work; see, Shou 51 and 52.

Note that the name of the Shou 'Assembly' never occurs in the text, although the idea of companies of spirits, ancestors, and fauna, is there. See the final paragraph of the commentary to Shou 32, multitude.

Shou 60
Tsan 532-540
CHI
To store

積

Yin guards the great closure;
Yang however, the small opening.

Mountains, streams, swamps, marshes;
The myriad things, to where they would return. *1/532*

Blackness storing nothing;
Making brightness the foundation. *2/533*

Storing, not using,
Achieves great use.
The knight attains a resolute heart. *3/534*

Storing stones, not food;
Wasting toil and labour. *4/535*

The knight stores up virtue,
Keeping in the carriage his ears. *5/536*

The granary is not full —
Robbed, not bare. *6/537*

Great fullness and ripeness are allotted to man;
New and fresh things are to come. *7/538*

The greatest and most colourful;
Jade, and many-coloured silks, arouse desires;
They beckon vagabonds and highwaymen. *8/539*

The humble man has nothing to store;
His achievements are in progeny and posterity. *9/540*

Shou 61
Tsan 541-549
SHIH
Adorn

飾

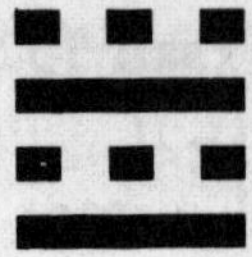

Words are neither words
Nor the use of words. 1/541

The sound of the yellow tongue
The splashes of the yellow brush;
There is advantage is seeing the one who knows. 2/542

There is advantage in babble —
The babble of discussion
Among the men who make forecasts. 3/543 4/544

Falling words are like water;
Their substance is by Heaven parted. 5/545

Words lacking practical help
Are a hindrance;
They fly past
The great man shaking as if by the wind. 6/546 7/547

No single word is trifling when spoken. 8/548

Look at the adornment above.

Frogs croak,
Gasping, gasping.
Blood comes out of their mouths. 9/549

飾

Notes

Although this Shou is entitled 'Adorn' much of the substance of this text concerns the spoken word. With reference to the last line, the expression 'to spit blood' (see Shou 10) means to slander.

'The great man shaking'. See a reference in the commentary to Shou 21.

Shou 62
Tsan 550-558
I
Doubt

疑

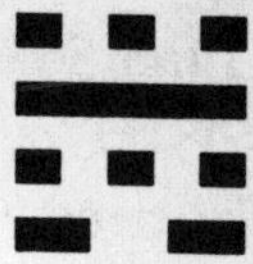

Yin and Yang grind against each other,
The elements completed,
Engraved in pairs;
As if existing,
As if not existing.

Doubting the magnitude of the sun's brightness;
Enduring thus, grieving, grieving. *1/550*

In his heart
His forebears. *2/551*

Doubt tests the old;
It happens, in this augury, there is confidence. *3/552*

Doubt tests the old;
The first thing to do is to ask. *4/553*

Red, yellow, doubt, metal, centre. *5/554*

Demons and the soul in doubt. *6/555*

Yelping, screeching:
The wooden spear in the bird;
An arrow shot into the fox;
Taking an eye and an ear;
Such is cruelty. *7/556-9/558*

疑

Notes

This Shou corresponds to the Autumn Equinox; see the section on the calendar, page 33.

'Red, yellow, doubt, metal, centre'. A reference to controversy over correct doctrine, according to the gloss. Curiously, the two principle sects of Tibetan Buddhists were to be known as the 'yellow' and the 'red' sects — a thousand years after Yang Hsiung.

Shou 63
Tsan 559-567
SHIH
Inspect

視

Yin completing: the mother's sister;
Yang completing: the deceased mother.
Its shape and form completed and united
It can be inspected.

Inside there is clarity;
No need for a light. *1/559*

Inside there is clarity;
The Self is deep, yet explored. *2/560*

Lesser people inspect the outside,
They are unable to see into the heart. *3/561 4/562*

Her forehead is heavily powdered;
Drench her face with water;
Wash her thoroughly with pure rain.
Then inspection will show it is not the younger sister. *5/563*

The Luan-bird and the Feng-bird;
If there is confusion,
Their virtues will be as clear radiance. *6/564*

The carriage appears;
The kingfisher hides;
It is best to go on foot outside. *7/565*

The cock and hen kingfishers flying in pairs;
Their wings shelter the fox. *8/566*

The mole's tail:
Personal rebellion. *9/567*

祝

Notes

The Luan-bird; the Feng-bird. These were fabulous birds whose appearance signified prosperity. The character for Luan includes the phonetic particle meaning 'tinkling bells' as on a horse's bridle or an emperor's carriage. A musical tone was given this name, because it was supposed to be at the same pitch as the Luan-bird's cry. It is sometimes translated as 'phoenix' but this term is more properly applied to the Feng-bird. Although the word Feng has a similar sound to the word 'phoenix' it is not usually thought that the two are related; the Chinese 'phoenix' had a male and female of the species, and there is no equivalent legend to the Feng building a nest on which it immolated itself — this being an essential part of the Western legend. The Feng may have been the Golden Pheasant.

There are two references to this Shou in the following Shou 64.

Dragon and Tiger, traditional symbols of Yang and Yin.

The Sea, water inundating,
Flowing as fast as flight.
Shou 76

Shou 64
Tsan 568-576
CH'EN
Sinking

沈

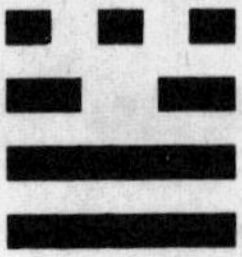

Yin enfolds Yang,
Yang enfolds Yin.
Ambition remains the Secret's function.

'Sinking' listens in the women's quarters;
Nothing audible is in the divination. *1/568*

'Sinking' inspects the Self;
It sees excellence
In shame and disgrace. *2/569*

Sinking in beauty;
Made deaf by the drumskins. *3/570*

Courtesy sinks in inspection.
Eating bitter food is the augury. *4/571*

Eagles and hawks soar aloft;
Sinking in the belly:
Good is the salamander,
Evil is the gruel. *5/572-7/574*

As if in pairs,
As if threading their way,
Barn owls and night owls,
Red flesh,
Oppressing. *8/575 9/576*

沈

Notes

This Shou is the beginning of the eighth *T'ien*, and thus corresponds to the first week of October, when Autumn is drawing on. There are two references to the previous Shou (63) 'Inspect' in the third and fifth verses; in fact, the three Shou 62, 63 and 64, form a series, even though they belong to different *T'ien*, with the numerous references to birds of prey — four in this Shou alone — hunting, and hunted animals. The idea of wings, and flight, is even carried over into the next shou, where Night is likened to a dark enveloping bird. There are further references to Shou 46 (Extending) through the word 'audible' and references to the sounds of drums.

The sixth verse is a model of how the most complex imagery can be resolved into a simple concept. The word which is here translated as 'salamander' is a character formed of the radicals for 'female' and 'frog'. It is a rare word, and the dictionaries which list it give Yang Hsiung's work as the source. Since the frog radical also appears in the character for a stove (see Shou 44), 'salamander' is a neat way of conveying the two kinds of imagery in this verse: that of the frog, and the stove used to cook the gruel in the last line of the verse. On the surface then, it would appear that the meaning of this verse is that a 'sinking in the belly' is due the gruel cooked on the stove. In actual fact it means nothing of the kind. Frogs, when they croak, puff themselves out; a female, when visibly puffed out, is pregnant. So it would *now* seem to be that the meaning of this verse is that the sinking feeling in the belly is good if due to pregnancy, but bad if due to eating poor food. But no! we next have to consider the 'eagles and hawks soaring aloft'. It is not physical pregnancy with which this verse is concerned; it is the development of ideas. 'Eagles and hawks soar aloft' means 'head in the clouds'; at last, the whole verse can be interpreted 'many ideas, but impracticable', or alternatively, 'the road to hell is paved with good intentions'. (See cross-references in Shou 32 and 77.)

Shou 65
Tsan 577-585
NEI
Within

内

The Dragon descends into the mud.
The Knight advantageously uses his grip. 1/577

Hard travelling;
Efforts injurious. 2/578

The enveloping dusk in flight
Folds within its wings
Desires that would fill a palace;
Yet no sight of the maiden. 3/579-5/581

Crumbling walls where weeds grow;
Yet this element is considered a blessing. 6/582 7/583

Rain falls upon the earth;
Never seeming to stop,
Never seeming to flood. 8/584 9/585

内

Notes

The Dragon (see Shou 1) symbolizes rains and floods, which are pictured in the last verse of this text. In this Shou, the character (物) which has been translated throughout this text as 'elements' in the sense of 'the symbolism and meaning of the Shou', has been altered, in later editions of the T'ai Hsüan, to (勿) meaning 'not'. This, of course, considerably alters the meaning of the fourth verse, though it is understandable that later commentators should imagine that 'crumbling walls where weeds grow' is *not* a blessing. It seems to me, however, that Yang Hsiung appears to be stressing the fact that what might appear to be decay is in fact to be 'classed as a blessing'.

Shou 66
Tsan 586-594
CH'Ü
Departing

去

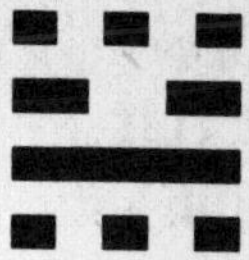

Yang departed makes Yin,
Yin departed makes Yang.
The elements are now united,
Unleashed and wild.

Departing from the son;
The father departing from the minister.

Life of the body
Departs on completion.

Heaven bequeaths them fame.

去

Notes

This text is too short to be divided into Tsan. Please see the remarks on page 55.

Shou 67
Tsan 595-603
HUI
Obscure

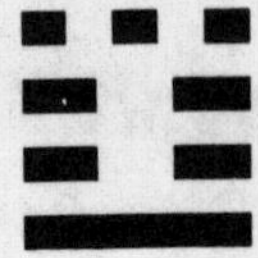

'Obscure' is a category.

The vermilion metal coffer.

The Sun is principal and Central;
The Moon is principal and surpassing.

The Knight, himself obscured,
Does not enter into poverty.

The Sun is Central, the Moon surpassing;
The brightness, fearful, is eclipsed.

The Sun's effulgence sends its brightness,
Doubtfully complying, on a journey.

Notes

The references here are to an eclipse of the Sun. 'Hui' not only means obscure, but also is a name given to the last day of the month, when the moon is dark (the Chinese month commencing, of course, with the new moon). This Shou would cover the days October 15-19; if the fifteenth of October were the last day of the Chinese month, then the previous Chinese New Year would have commenced on December 22; I think that this is further evidence for believing that Yang Hsiung intended the calendar to begin with the Winter Solstice. 'Vermilion' although red, is sometimes used to mean silver, associated in Western alchemy with the Moon (as in 'lunar caustic' — silver nitrate). The 'Vermilion metal coffer' might therefore allude to the eclipse. Eclipses of the Sun can only occur when the moon is 'dark', that is, at the time of the new moon.

There is a further important note in the calendar section on page 35. This Shou has been considered to be too short for division into Tsan.

Shou 68
Tsan 604-612
MENG
Dimmed

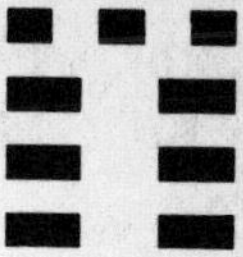

Eyesight dimmed.
Divisions:
Getting brighter.

Heaven does not inspect its boundaries.

A metal mirror is the divination.

There is no delusion for the man who is wealthy.

Notes

'Dimmed' here means 'eyesight obscured'. The imagery continues from the previous Shou, which is total eclipse. Here the eclipse is passing. The metal mirror was a symbol of the Universe; many examples of the Han dynasty survive; their backs usually portray a square within a circle, often surrounded by symbols representing the twelve months of the year, the four quarters of the earth, and other astronomical devices.

This Shou, too, is really too short for division into Tsan.

Shou 69
Tsan 613-621
CH'IUNG
Poverty

窮

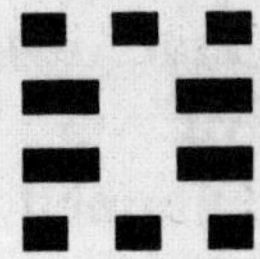

Poverty contemplating: intelligence.
That which is taught remains in the heart. *1/613*

Earth is not in harmony;
The wooden stalks are long and narrow . . . *2/614 3/615*

Beauty lacking restraint —
In the bowels danger, danger;
No error in the edicts. *4/616 5/617*

Fording the stream;
Frost and snow;
Wound about the neck
A scarf halter. *6/618 7/619*

The broken jade ring;
The smashed jade tablet;
The ancient stove;
Beef and edible frogs. *8/620*

Heaven sends calamities through them. *9/621*

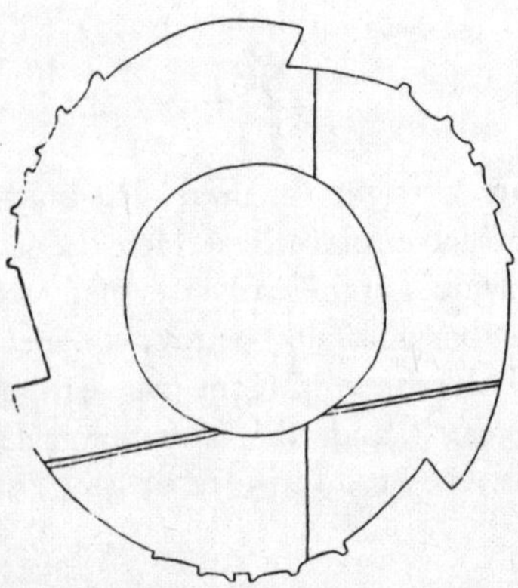

窮

Notes

That which one has taught to someone was regarded as the third of the 'three imperishables', the others being one's virtue, and one's meritorious achievements. 'The Earth not in harmony' is a reference to the diagram itself; note that there are reflecting pairs of doubly and triply broken lines, but no unbroken lines.

The 'stove' in the fifth verse refers to Shou 49. This verse also mentions two ancient ceremonial objects, the jade 'Pi' (regarded as a symbol of Heaven, but which may have anciently been an astronomical template), and the ancestral tablets (see further mentions in Shou 57 and 59).

Ch'en Jen Hsi remarks that verse 4 refers to long imprisonment.

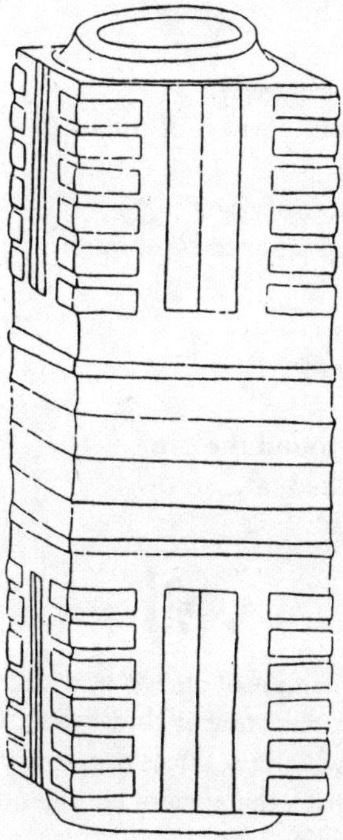

Shou 70
Tsan 622-630
KO
Hacking off

割

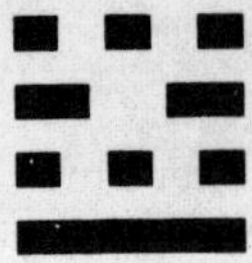

Hacking off the ears and eyes
Reaches into the heart and bowels. 1/622

Hacking off the tumours and goitres;
Advantageous for these to be lacking. 2/623 3/624

Hacking off the nose:
Food in the mouth;
Losing the polypus. 4/625

Hacking off part of the tumour:
Furs for one of a pair of horses. 5/626

Hacking lacking creativity:
Sated from the four corners of the earth. 6/627

Hacking lacking creativity:
The Way may not seem to be enough. 7/628

The spiny murex
Discusses the clouds. 8/629

The bright halo round the sun:
Sickness not hacked off. 9/630

割

Notes

This is an interesting example of 'image' and 'divination' text; note that every verse of the text, except one, includes the title character. The spiny murex is the shellfish which produces the deep purple dye used for the robes of Roman emperors: the ancient commentary adds the note that this is an augury of fine weather!

Shou 71
Tsan 631-639
CHIH
Stop

Stop by the bare trees;
Plead for the cause of poverty. *1/631*

The pillars determine the roof of the building;
In such a way, the hub determines the wheel of the
chariot. *2/632 3/633*

The square rotating, the corners pivoted;
Misfortune is the bottom of a carriage. *4/634*

The carriage winds about its rugged way;
The horse's mane, and its hooves. *5/635*

The bow shall the virtuous turn back;
The bow shall the evil turn back. *6/636*

The virtuous horse rages;
The evil horse rages. *7/637 8/638*

Snapped is the fully stretched bow;
Broken is the carriage;
Finally, no pretence. *9/639*

Notes

The title of this Shou, Stop, appears only as the first character of the entire text, although there are two entirely different kinds of image, the carriage and the bow, used here. The word 'bare' is a translation of 'T'ung' which although Shou 12 (Boy) has the alternative sense given here. This Shou, after all, corresponds to the first week of November, when leaves would have fallen, and poverty would begin to stare the less fortunate in the face.*

The second and third verses have an astrological-cosmological significance. As in Shou 69, there is no unbroken line in the diagram.

*Poverty, of course, recalls Shou 69.

Shou 72
Tsan 640-648
CHIEN
Obduracy

堅

Yin's shape pitted by the light of the Sun;
Yang in furs and silk.
This element indicates quarrels, obduracy, violence.

'Obduracy' is white jade;
Its shape, however, may be transformed. *1/640 2/641*

Obduracy is not chaste;
Doubt is dispersed from the centre. *3/642 4/643*

Obduracy is not chaste;
Neither is it able to remain even and unfirom. *5/644*

Little bees building, building;
A rainbow from their shimmering, shimmering.
No trifling matter. *6/645 7/646*

Remaining obdurate is the rainbow;
The shimmering (is the State);
The Great Rainbow (is virtue);
Little falsehoods. *8/647 9/648*

堅

Notes

It is difficult to reconcile the image of obduracy (likened to white jade) with changeability, yet twice we are told that this is in fact what is intended. It appears that the last verse is an extension of the penultimate one, and that the ancient glosses have completed what may have been a fragmentary text. Certainly the idea of the State having as much substance as the shimmering appearance of the wings of thousands of busy insects makes a good deal of sense; these later additions are therefore given in parentheses.

Their diligence, their diligence,
Enfolds the carriage,
Enters the abyss,
Turns back on the boat,
Ascends the mountain.
Shou 80

Shou 73
Tsan 649-657
CH'ENG
Completing

成

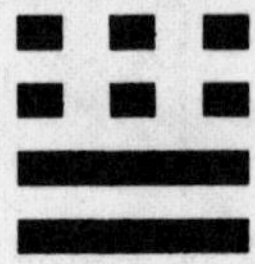

Completion draws in its coils of dazzling brightness;
Completion flies, but there is no pursuit.
The Centre and Completion alone survey the Great.

成

Notes

The final T'ien begins with this extremely short text; a terse statement of the beginning and end of the T'ai Hsüan.

The opening lines draw a very vivid picture of a spiral galaxy, describing a universe, swirling with incalculable force into space, flinging out into the vastness, yet without pursuit. Yang Hsiung could have known nothing of the structure of the universe, let alone the existence of spiral galaxies, so it is all the more astonishing that this brief text should be so extraordinarily perceptive.

Note that this diagram has two triply broken lines, and two unbroken ones, representing the opposite forces of T'ien and Ti, without the central, Jen, force. The inherent cosmology is not overlooked in the text, as brief as it is.*

Being so short, it is not divided into Tsan. See the remarks on page 55.

*I.e. 'Centre' means the *T'ien* commencing with Shou 1, Centre (Shou 1-9), and 'Completion' (in the third line) means the *T'ien* commencing with this Shou (Shou 73-81). Shou 1-9 are T'ien forces, Shou 73-81 Ti forces; this is how the tetragram has been interpreted in the third line of text.

Shou 74
Tsan 658-666
CHIH
Will

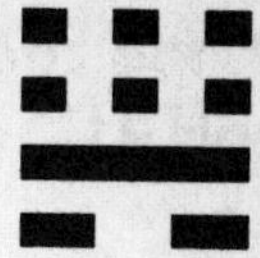

Yin and Yang are exchanged,
Stumbling upon each other,
The door-leaf completed.

One is calamity;
Weeping silently,
The myriad things.

Without a partition in the Will,
One is two.

Notes

This is a 'philosophical' statement, without any augury save that of the 'calamity, weeping silently' which seems somehow to have slipped in to this mystical statement.

Compare Shou 16 (Exchange) where Yin is exchanged for Yang, and vice versa, and also Shou 14 (Sharpness), which contains the statement 'One is, but not two'. Note that this does not mean 'by dividing one, we obtain two', but that in order to perceive the difference between 'one' and 'two', or for that matter any two things, one has to understand the nature of each.

This very short text has not been divided into Tsan; see the remarks on page 55.

Shou 75
Tsan 667-675
SHIH
Error

失

Yin: greatly making rebellion,
Yang is not able to achieve.
This element is sinking,
It is unfathomable.

Slashing at falsity,
Destruction with a knife;
The yellow infant. 1/667

By means of the Centre
There is luxuriant growth. 2/668

Through the Knight,
Misdemeanours are pardoned. 3/669

Full is the granary, dense are the fields,
Food in abundance;
Left untended the foundations. 4/670

Sickness; consequence: medicine.
The wizard; consequence: potions. 5/671 6/672

Hens cackling at early morning;
Meat, fish, and wood. 7/673

Days and months pass away;
The corpse decays and changes. 8/674

Changes in the corpse,
Yet it is not sent away. 9/675

失

Notes

The explanation of the first verse lies in the diagram; three triply broken lines sandwiching an unbroken one. Many of these images have been used before; the wizard (shaman, or witch-doctor) in Shou 51. To the seventh verse is added the commentary that a mythical, extremely timid, creature is indicated, the symbolism being two people who are afraid of each other. Ch'en Jen Hsi suggests that 'yellow infant' means an old man.

The curious imagery of the corpse in the last two verses can be possibly explained by the fact that Shih, Error, and Shih, a corpse, would have had almost identical pronunciations. (See Shou 32.)

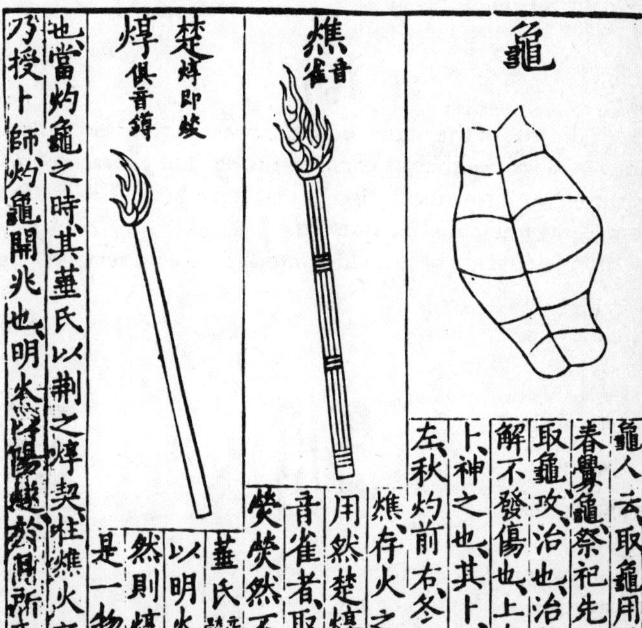

Shou 76
Tsan 676-684
CHÜ
Troubles

劇

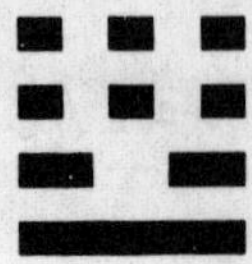

To come out of the wild,
To see the wilderness,
To have the tiger tend the pig,
To hitch up the trousers because of floods.

The Sea; water inundating,
Flowing as fast as flight,
Finally, unable to speak of it.

劇

Notes

Although the title of the Shou does not appear in this very short text, it is interesting to see that its components do. The character for Chü is made from the elements for tiger, a pig, and a knife. The image is of someone being inundated by troubles.

This short test has not been divided into Tsan; see the remarks on page 55.

Shou 77
Tsan 586-693
HSÜN
Domesticated

馴

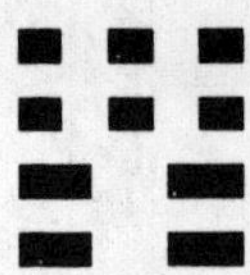

The pregnant women has rich food.
Daughter and son toil away,
No tranquility their fate.

馴

Notes

See the commentary to Shou 64 for a remarkable note about the word Yang Hsiung uses for 'pregnant'. The title of the Shou does not appear in this very brief text. The diagram is interesting: two doubly, and two triply broken lines; the reverse of Shou 45. See the remarks regarding division into Tsan on page 55.

Shou 78
Tsan 694-702
CHIANG
Taking

將

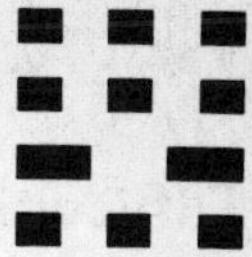

Taken in flying,
Having obtained wings.
Advantage in rising up to Heaven. *1/694 2/695*

A great number of little birds
Are taken in flying.
Plucking their quills,
Tail and wings.
Suppose the multitude did not get such substance. *3/396 4/397*

Galloping boats, sailing carriages;
Their destruction not far off. *5/698*

A tiny child:
The hundred clans remain in the abyss. *6/699*

The senior elder:
Scattering the boats. *7/700*

Red silkworms climb the withered mulberry bush.
Their cocoons are not yellow. *8/701 9/702*

將

Notes

'The hundred clans' is an expression meaning 'all people generally'. They remain in oblivion, or darkness. 'Abyss' is frequently used throughout the T'ai Hsüan as the antithesis of exalted, or even Heaven. 'Their cocoons are not yellow' i.e. do not ripen, because there are no leaves on the bush for the worms to eat. Silkworms appear in Shou 35, the 'hundred clans' in Shou 42, boats and carts in Shou 28 and 80.

Shou 79
Tsan 703-711
NAN
Difficulties

難

The egg breaks
The stone infertile. 1/703

The great wagon
lumbers on, lumbers on. 2/704 3/705

Upwards, hauling up the mountain,
Downwards, braking against the stream. 4/706

Uprooting stones for precious gems,
Strength dwindling,
Help needed. 5/707 6/708

Striking the stones,
Breaking open
The wooden bands. 7/709 8/710

Splitting flesh. 9/711

難

Notes

Most of the images here are of 'breaking open' whether an egg, or a stone. The title of the Shou does not appear itself, though it is inferred in the idea of difficulties. It is used only once elsewhere in the T'ai Hsüan, as the final character in the opening verse of Shou 3, 'Laboriously slowly'. The commentary to that Shou alludes to the fact that this is the third Shou from the end, just as 'Slowly' is the third from the beginning. The second lines of the second and third verses each use the character Ch'uan (巛) Streams, to mean long and arduous travelling. The sense in the third verse is the difficulty of hauling a wagon up a mountain, and the equally difficult job of holding it back while it descends a steep hill. The title of this Shou, Nan, is also the name of some kind of bird, which probably suggested the image of eggs breaking.

Shou 80
Tsan 712-720
CH'IN
Diligent

勤

Great Yin freezing solid;
Fearful of taking the first step outside
To penetrate Yang's abode.

Obscurity;
Putting one's back into the task. *1/712*

Toil possesses grace,
Diligence — control, control.
The Knight possesses the Centre. *2/713 3/714*

A noose;
My flesh is myself. *4/715*

Their silent sobbing, weeping, weeping,
Vermilion becoming,
The string of coins wounding. *5/716*

Diligence possesses complete merit,
Almost from Heaven. *6/717*

Alone, toil does not achieve;
Their nose-to-tail practices. *7/718*

Their diligence, their diligence,
Enfolds the carriage,
Enters the abyss,
Turns back on the boat,
Ascends the mountain. *8/719 9/720*

勤

Notes

'Great Yin freezing solid'. This Shou corresponds to the middle of December.

Shou 81
Tsan 721-729
YANG
Nourishing

養

Yin — a fully stretched bow in the wilderness;
Yang — the mysterious myriad things
Glowing crimson beneath.

Hoarded in the heart of the abyss;
Wonderful is the intellect's foundation. 1/721

Hoarded in the heart of the abyss,
The mind outside it. 2/722

Feasting, eating:
Regulations, regulations;
Their purposes dependent, dependent.
Advantageous to levy taxes on purchases. 3/723

The yellow heart sits in the belly.
The white breast gives life to flesh.
Trust in virtue, not in making amends. 4/724

The yellow heart sits in the belly.
Rising, it attains Heaven. 5/725

Scrupulously, scrupulously,
One day, three sacrifices;
The ox is the omen:
A plump one is not advantageous. 6/726

Scrupulously, scrupulously,
The sacrifice is plump,
But without a body. 7/727

The little child hauls an elephant;
The married lady and the man:
Honour and courage;
The Knight nourishes the sick. 8/728

Fishbones do not rid the poison.
The sickness begins with ghosts
On the top of the mound. 9/729

* * *

The stars, like the years,
Repeatedly return to their beginning.

The stars, like the years,
Repeatedly return to their end.

Now all is frozen;
Hands reverently lift the crimson disc up to Heaven.
There, in the clear sky,
Is the Mystery's secret fountain.

養

Notes

Appropriately, the final text of the T'ai Hsüan is the longest and most comprehensive, including philosophical statements, little homilies, sybilline verses with interpretations, and a reassuring conclusion. This Shou is distinguished from all the others by having 'philosophical' verses at the end, so bringing the whole work to a satisfactory close. Note the name of this Shou: Yang. Is this a concidence again, or perhaps another deliberate literary conceit on Yang's own name, as is perhaps the case with Shou 19?

The 'crimson' of the first verse is the Sun, which appears fiery red in Winter, and is hidden for most of the day 'in the abyss'. The final verse recalls the first, and refers to a ritual act of lifting a solar disc — probably the sacred Pi — to Heaven. In the clear winter sky the Sun begins its journey anew, like the stars in their courses, like the everlasting cycles of days, months, years, and dynasties 'repeatedly returning to their beginning, repeatedly returning to their end'.

Ghosts, or demons, Kuei (鬼) were regarded as responsible for disease.

PART THREE:
THE T'AI HSÜAN CHING AND SCIENTIFIC THOUGHT

Introduction

Yang Hsiung's hypothesis that the dual principle of Yin and Yang could be complemented by a third force was a brilliant concept equivalent to the discovery of zero. It was, in his time, a heresy, like those arguments over dogma that have plagued the world's religions for centuries. Nor was it an easy hypothesis to accept; the notion of Yin and Yang was far too ingrained into the Chinese mind by Yang Hsiung's time. Oddly enough, it was the exact converse of the situation in the West, where the Trinity was accepted as a part of the Christian dogma, and it was the dualists who were the heretics. But perhaps if the adherents of the T'ai Hsüan had been martyred for their beliefs their philosophy might have acquired notoriety — and perhaps wider circulation. As it turned out, it was largely ignored and regarded as no more than a curiosity by most of the Taoist philosophers who took the trouble to study it.

Even Yang Hsiung himself found it difficult to cast off the idea of Yin and Yang, as we can see from most of the opening verses of the 81 Shou. This may have been the main reason why the T'ai Hsüan failed to be accepted as a totally new concept, and instead was regarded as an unnecessary appendage to existing philosophies. There may be a quite understandable reason for Yang Hsiung's temerity. Though he was well aware of the short-comings of the Yin-Yang, there is a curious clue in one of his writings: '*I have studied the rise and fall of the (Chou) I . . .*' The *fall* of the I? The fact that he was writing about the fall of the I has to be taken in parallel with his belief that there was no greater work among the classics. He must have felt interest in the I to be declining, and that by writing the T'ai Hsüan he hoped to add a new dimension to the I and stimulate fresh interest in what was to him the greatest work of antiquity.

For a new dimension is what he certainly did add to the I. The notion of a 'trinity' was not altogether unknown or new to Yang Hsiung; the *Li Chi* (Record of Rites) has a clear definition of the 'tripartite' nature of divine inspiration.* This work would certainly be known to Yang Hsiung, since the core of the work had been written about half a century before (that is, between 70 and 50 BC) and although its later passages were written at about the end of the first century (some fifty years after the death of Yang Hsiung) there are passages in it which are anterior to Confucius, and perhaps even older than the I itself.

The T'ai Hsüan is a Universal theory — not an explanation of the Universe or its origins, but a method of reasoning to account for the existence and behaviour of everything within the universe. It is far more scientifically elegant than the dual principle of Yin and Yang, or the binary system of Leibniz that has come to be the universal means of communication in the modern world of electronics and computers. Yin and Yang became negative and positive; and negative and positive answered for No and Yes. So sophisticated has modern electronics become, with ever-increasing, apparently limitless scope, that it is easy to be deluded into thinking that an application of the binary system could encompass all thought — as was Leibniz's original proposition. But it is self-limiting. It is like a tangled mass of wire that can be shaped into an infinite number of different forms — but will always look like a mass of wire. No matter how many times a line is divided by two, it will never be divided into three. If, by a process of bisection, we continued to try to divide such a line, we would eventually reach a point just a little to the right, or the left, of the mark which would show one third of the line. And we could close this gap still further by dividing it into two; and the gap that was left could be closed still more, but the exact spot would never be reached.

The idea that all thought, and all matter, all universal laws, even, can be expressed in terms of Yes and No is almost instinctive to the scientific mind. It is this which has made the Yin-Yang theory so readily acceptable. But it is a fetter; it blocks the creation of new ideas, and ultimately clogs the progress of knowledge. The next few pages look at some of the ways in which the T'ai Hsüan is far better equipped than the Yin Yang to deal with scientific concepts, and how it can even open doors to the creation of new ideas.

The T'ai Hsüan and Scientific Thought

Apologists for the I Ching often place great emphasis on the importance of the coincidental parallels between the Liang I (the two forces Yin and

*'In the beginning was the Mysterious Unity, Miao I, distinguished in three principles: Heaven, Intelligence, and Spirit.' (Preface to the *Li Chi*.)

Yang) and the electromagnetic nature of the physical universe — that is, the attraction between like, and the repulsion by unlike, forces of magnetism and electricity, as if this in some way shows that the electromagnetic forces had been anticipated in Chinese philosophy some thousands of years before their scientific acceptance in the West. Unfortunately the two systems are not at all analogous. The nearest approach that the Yin-Yang makes to Western scientific thinking is in an altogether different field concerning not the *forces* in the universe, but its *constituent parts*.

Since Yin and Yang were regarded as divisions of the T'ai Chi (太極) the Great Unity, and in turn were the parents from which the 'ten thousand things' Wan Wu (萬物) were engendered, it is clear that Yin and Yang are what would be known to Aristotle as 'elements'. Conversely, the five so-called elements of Chinese science (wood, earth, metal, water, and fire), were not regarded as the *ingredients* of matter (as Aristotleans regarded air, earth, fire, and water), but the *manifestations* of matter.

But there is another serious flaw in the dualist theory of Chinese philosophy — the very concept that Yang Hsiung, despite his admiration for the I Ching, was at pains to try and correct. In presupposing that all things are either Yin, Yang, or a mixture of both, the dualist theory precludes that which is neither (how this restricted kind of thinking has led to the most extraordinary paradoxes in mathematics will be dealt with later). And while Yin and Yang may have certain parallels with the negative and positive forces of electromagnetism, they fail to take account of that other all-prevading force, gravity, which does not have positive and negative natures, only a single, attracting one. Does a body falling through gravity show the effect of Greater Yang attracting Lesser Yang, or is it Greater Yin attracting lesser Yin? The question is academic, for it cannot be satisfactorily answered. Paradox, or false logic? But where the Yin-Yang theory fails to provide a solution, the T'ai Hsüan succeeds, for it teaches that between the extremes of the T'ien and Ti lies a third force, the Jen. The T'ai Hsüan would explain gravity as, not an attractive force between T'ien and Ti, but the central attractive and reciprocal force which acts on Jen. We shall see shortly how this central, attractive Jen force is able to explain other important features of atomic structure.

It would be facile to use the terminology of the T'ai Hsüan to explain away such phenomena as solid, liquid and gas, by saying that the former was Ti, Earth, and therefore solid; gas was tenuous, and filled the heavens, therefore it was T'ien, while liquid, which was obviously not a combination of gas and solid, but an independent state, must therefore be Jen. This does not tell us anything new.

The T'ai Hsüan, in Shou 2, tells us 'The creation of things begins by assembling them into groups'. All scientific knowledge is based upon observation and classification; *but categorization which does not lead to conclusion is sterile*: the Liang I (the system of Yin and Yang) may be an inexhaustible system of classification, but it does not generate *new* knowledge.

The T'ai Hsüan, however, does lead to the creation of new paths of exploration. Take for example the joining of an atom of sodium with an atom of chlorine to form a molecule of common salt. Common salt has neither the properties of the highly reactive metal sodium, which bursts into flames on touching water, nor the choking green and corrosive gas, chlorine. Superficially, we could say that the 'Ti' sodium and the 'T'ien' chlorine had together formed the 'Jen' salt. To understand why this happens, one has to look into the atom itself. There are three main observable particles in the atom (observable being used here, of course, in the widest sense of the word) the electron, with negligible mass (weight) but carrying a single negative electric charge; the neutron, which has mass but no charge, and the proton, which has both a positive charge, and a mass. The orbiting electron is T'ien;* the charge on the proton, opposite to it must be Ti; yet it has mass, so it must be Jen also. This actually leads to a deduction: that there must be some particles, Ti, which have a positive charge but no mass; and other particles, Jen + T'ien, which have a mass and an electrical negative charge.

Although attempts to equate Yin and Yang with the negative and positive forces of electromagnetism soon lead into murky backwaters, the superficial resemblance of the two forces to the sexes has lead to a biological interpretation, another erroneous analogy which is no less full of pitfalls. The similarity of the forces of Yin and Yang to the phenomenon of male

*I was asked by Dr Anneliese Bulling, the noted authority on Chinese symbolism, why it was that I equated the electron, which has a negative charge, with the T'ien force; T'ien always being regarded as positive. The reason belongs to the nature of the electron itself, which is in movement round the anchored nucleus of the atom. There is nothing actually 'positive' or 'negative' about particles; it so happens, that like the poles of the magnet, they have equal and opposite forces, and the terms 'negative and positive' were originally applied as a convenient form of terminology. They might just have easily been called 'black and white'. In the early days of electrical science, it was thought that the electric current flowed from the positive terminal of the battery to the negative. It is now accepted that the current flow is in fact the other way round, and that it is the 'electron' flow which shows the true direction of the electric current. Consequently, the term T'ien accurately applies to the electron. In the miniature cosmogony of the atom, the central nucleus is the Earth, Ti, the surrounding electron cloud its T'ien, Heaven. The terminology is practical, not mystical.

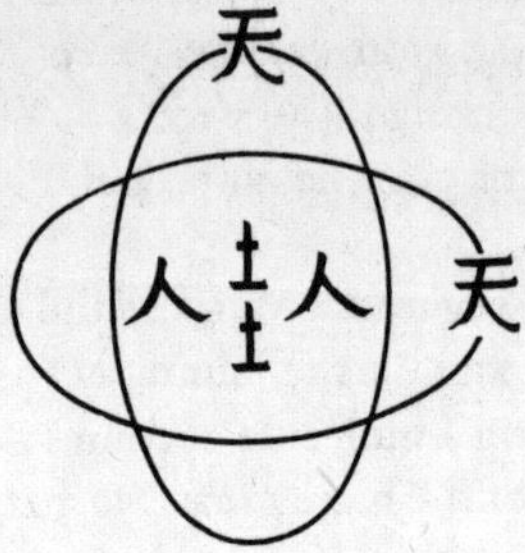

Atom of Helium

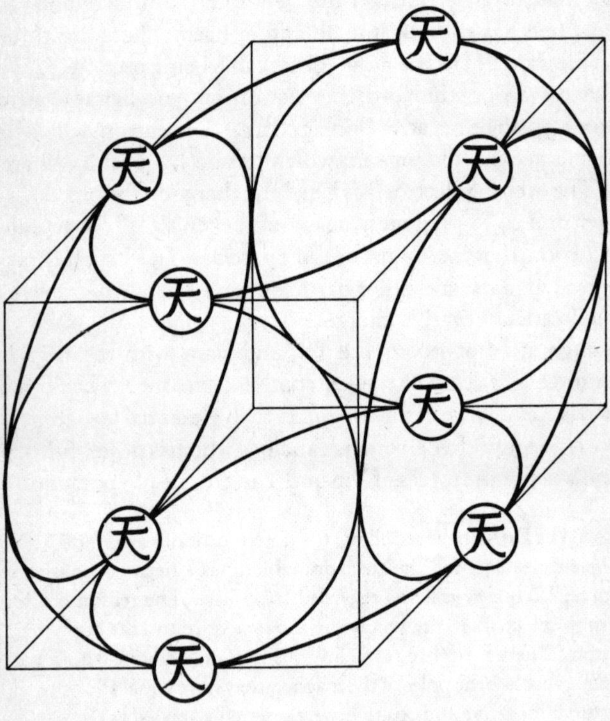

Diagram of Outer Shell of an atom of Neon.

1. The Helium atom. In conventional terms, two neutrons and two protons are orbited by two electrons. In the terms of the T'ai Hsüan, two T'ien particles, two Jen, and two Ti, each balance the others, thus producing an 'inert' element.
2. The Neon atom. At the centre of the atom is the nucleus (not shown). Orbiting it are ten electrons; the outer eight balancing each other exactly, like the corners of a cube, thus producing a completely stable, or 'inert' element.

and female is so evident that it is easy to forget that the attraction between the sexes is by no means as predictable as the attraction between unlike poles of a magnet. *All* north poles attract *all* south poles; if life were as easy as that! Nor should one forget that only a proportion of the living things on this planet have two distinct sexual forms. We need not travel to outer galaxies to find creatures with but one sex, three sexes, or no sexes at all; we have but to look at the myriad protozoa, self-reproducing plants, the monosexual gastropods, and the complex life-cycles of the flowering plants (which require the intermediary assistance of a creature from an altogether different life-form) to find organisms every bit as alien as the most imaginative creations of science fiction. The spirogyra, banded snail, and horse-chestnut, know not the Yin and Yang.

The terms Yin and Yang have also been applied to the recessive and dominant genes in genetic studies; but exchanging one set of terms for another teaches nothing new. It makes no difference to the observation whether albinism in rabbits is due to Yin genes or recessive ones. More significantly, it takes no account of the creation of new species, which is the whole purpose of breeding, whether the subject is a racing pigeon or winter rice. But replace the terms Yin and Yang by Ti and T'ien, and immediately there is the expectation of a third, unpredictable force, Jen, stepping in. The 'sports' of nature, the development of new species, is now accounted for.

In music, the phenomenon of the three poles, Ti, Jen and T'ien is particularly marked. Practically all Western music, from about the sixteenth century onwards, has been dominated by the feature of 'key-relationships'. Melodic lines, and the whole shape of symphonic structures, are based on the relative positions of three tonal centres: the tonic, and its dominant and sub-dominant keys. It is obvious that these relationships can be immediately equated to the balance of Ti and T'ien, the sub-dominant and dominant keys, with that of Jen, the tonic (all other related keys, as Schönberg points out, can be seen as functions of the dominant or sub-dominant). The function of the key, or tonality, of a passage of music may refer to the entire piece, or just a few bars, or even one chord. The remarkable feature is that tonality was an unknown feature in music in the time of Yang Hsiung! The mechanics of a theory of music were there, but had to wait for fifteen hundred years before they were applied.

So far, we have only been looking at tangible evidence of the application of the T'ai Hsüan to various branches of science. Our next incursion takes us into the rarified and vexatious byways of mathematics. This should be the most precise and logical of all the disciplines, but it appears that even mathematics can become hopelessly entangled when trying to solve some of the problems of its own creation.

First of all, it is necessary to consider the whole process of mathematics from an entirely new viewpoint, as if the subject had just been invented. Two illustrations will serve to show the problems of the relationships between numbers. If we take a pair of scales, and put one pound weight into the left hand pan, and a pound weight into the other, the two weights balance. The total weight is two pounds; and yet, if we tip each pan with the finger, it will seem to have no weight: it is balanced by the other weight. Which of the weights is negative, in order to counter balance the other? For if each pan has no weight, but the two weights together equal two, then $1-1=1+1$. But neither of the weights has a minus quality; both are 'positive' weights; $1+1=0$; and hence, at the point of balance, $0=2$. The Jen force is both the summation, and the balance between T'ien and Ti forces.

The other concept to consider is that of two rooms; one has a chair, the other does not. The chair is removed, and taken away. Are both rooms now the same? The answer must be No; for while neither room has a chair, one of the rooms is *lacking* a chair which the other room never had. That is to say, $1-1\neq 0$.

These two concepts introduce the idea of a positive force acting upon, and neutralizing, a negative one, and vice versa. If we say, a positive thing and a negative thing together produce nothing, what has become of both these entities? It is useless to argue that the negative thing does not exist, for if it did not exist it would have no power to neutralize the positive. 1, and -1, are both entities; so $1-1=2$. In such equations, two balancing forces are together twice the original force.

Positive and negative concepts do not enter into the T'ai Hsüan; there are Ti qualities; and T'ien qualities. Together they produce Jen.

If bricks are put together in the shape of a house, a house exists which did not exist before. Again, as Shou 2 tells us: 'the creation of things begins by assembling them into groups'. What we can learn from the T'ai Hsüan is the concept of a set of numbers which represent the balance between two opposing forces, Jen, which is the balance between two equal opposites.* In conventional mathematics, there is a perplexing problem in dealing with the multiplication of negative numbers: -2×-2 gives, not -4, but $+4$. The problem is compounded when one tries to recall the roots of these numbers. If we square -2, the answer is 4. But what

*To take another example from the structure of the atom: some elements, the rare gases, argon, neon, krypton and the rest, are completely stable, and never combine with other elements. The reason for this stability is that their outside 'shell' of orbiting electrons is complete, having 8 electrons. 8 is the number of vertices in a cube; equal to $2+2+2+2$; reducing to (2)+(2), which further reduces to Jen: complete balance, and hence, total stability.

is the square root of –4? If the number –4 can be obtained by a process of subtraction in conventional mathematics, why cannot it be reached via a process of division?

Conventional mathematics tries to solve this paradox by the invention of an imaginary number *i* (called, predictably, the imaginary number) which is regarded as the square root of –1. There is no need here to go into the details of how this is used to explain the square root of –4; the square roots of minus numbers can be visualized quite easily on graph paper. The diagram below shows how both positive (T'ien) zero (Jen) and negative integers (Ti) have absolute values, and how simply a new mathematical notation could solve such paradoxes.

The opposite of zero is infinity; mathematicians have often speculated on whether there is only one infinity, or a number of them. An article in the 'Daily Telegraph' June 14 1982, prompted a reader* to comment 'If we accept Cantor's Continuum Theorem, which shows that infinities come in different sizes, then one must presume equally that there could be two zeros, one of which is smaller than the other, which is plainly absurd.'

*S.A.C. Fairfield, of Cambridge.

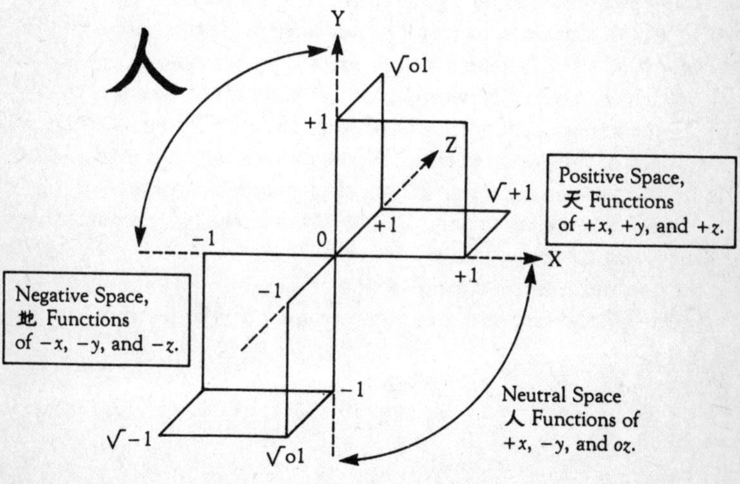

Graph of x, y, z, co-ordinates, showing the relationship of positive and negative real numbers to the neutral numbers.

Which it isn't; as we have seen, the T'ai Hsüan ternary view of mathematics admits a whole reckoning of zeros. But to illustrate it more tangibly, one can picture a circle being divided into progressively smaller pieces. If it is divided into two semi-circles, then multiplying one of these areas by two will once again produce the circle. If divided into a thousand portions, one of these thousandths, multiplied a thousand times, will again restore the circle. But divide it an infinite number of times, and the portions which are left are, according to conventional mathematical reasoning, equal to 0. If each of these poritions has no value, then it would be impossible, no matter how often it was multiplied, to restore the circle, or any portion of it. For nothing, no matter how often it is doubled, can ever produce something. It is clear that the absurdity lies in believing that zero, and infinity, are absolute numbers. Rather, there are indeed two absolute numbers; absolute infinity, which encompasses the whole universe, and absolute zero, which is total non-existence. But these two absolute numbers cannot be found by dividing a finite, or bounded, number a limitless number of times.

Finally, arising out of mathematical paradoxes, are the paradoxes of words, numbers, and logic. A vast tome, which has achieved some popularity, is the book '*Gödel-Escher-Bach*' by Douglas R. Hofstadter. Virtually the whole of the reasoning of this monumental work stems from the Epimenides paradox, 'All Cretans are liars; I am a Cretan therefore I lie; therefore I must be telling the truth.' There is of course, no paradox; if all Cretans *were* liars, he would never have made the statement. The statement is false in the first place, but it is an example of how simple it is to confuse absurdity with paradox. The kinds of paradoxes which Hofstadter introduces and develops are those which logicians would call 'the fallacy of the excluded middle'. The danger, which is evident from his attempts to bewilder, would have been avoided if only philosophers could train themselves to consider that between the two extremes there is always a third force, Jen.

Progress continues by the interaction of T'ien and Ti, but only Jen can change the direction, add the unknown quantity, and create.

APPENDIX

INDEX OF ENGLISH SHOU TITLES

INDEX OF CHINESE SHOU TITLES

INDEX OF CHINESE SHOU TITLES ARRANGED IN ORDER OF THEIR RADICALS

The Magic Squares of the 729 Tsan

Any row or column in these 9 arrangements of numbers adds up to the same total: 3,285. Furthermore, if these nine squares are placed on top of each other, then any column of figures from top to bottom also adds up to 3,285. Not only that, but any diagonal which passes through the central point of the cube also totals 3,285. Moreover, the outside faces, as well as certain other squares, have the curious property of producing this number from any regular pattern of nine numbers. Most important of all is that the centre number of the central square is 365; the number of days in the year, round which the calendar, and the T'ai Hsüan, revolve.

543	179	616	252	689	397	33	470	106
107	544	180	617	244	690	398	34	471
472	108	545	172	618	245	691	399	35
36	473	100	546	173	619	246	692	400
401	28	474	101	547	174	620	247	693
685	402	29	475	102	548	175	621	248
249	686	403	30	476	103	549	176	613
614	250	687	404	31	477	104	541	177
178	615	251	688	405	32	469	105	542

Top Layer.

97	534	170	607	324	680	388	24	461
462	98	535	171	608	316	681	389	25
26	463	99	536	163	609	317	682	390
391	27	464	91	537	164	610	318	683
684	392	19	465	92	538	165	611	319
320	676	393	20	466	93	539	166	612
604	321	677	394	21	467	94	540	167
168	605	322	678	395	22	468	95	532
533	169	606	323	679	396	23	460	96

2.

452	88	525	242	598	315	671	379	15
16	453	89	526	243	599	307	672	380
381	17	454	90	527	235	600	308	673
674	382	18	455	82	528	236	601	309
310	675	383	10	456	83	529	237	602
603	311	667	384	11	457	84	530	238
239	595	312	668	385	12	458	85	531
523	240	596	313	669	386	13	459	86
87	524	241	597	314	670	387	14	451

3.

6	443	160	516	233	589	306	662	370
371	7	444	161	517	234	590	298	663
664	372	8	445	162	518	226	591	299
300	665	373	9	446	154	519	227	592
593	301	666	374	1	447	155	520	228
229	594	302	658	375	2	448	156	521
522	230	586	303	659	376	3	449	157
158	514	231	587	304	660	377	4	450
442	159	515	232	588	305	661	378	5

4.

361	78	434	151	507	224	580	297	653
654	362	79	435	152	508	225	581	289
290	655	363	80	436	153	509	217	582
583	291	656	364	81	437	145	510	218
219	584	292	657	365	73	438	146	511
512	220	585	293	649	366	74	439	147
148	513	221	577	294	650	367	75	440
441	149	505	222	578	295	651	368	76
77	433	150	506	223	579	296	652	369

Central Layer.

725	352	69	425	142	498	215	571	288
280	726	353	70	426	143	499	216	572
573	281	727	354	71	427	144	500	208
209	574	282	728	355	72	428	136	501
502	210	575	283	729	356	64	429	137
138	503	211	576	284	721	357	65	430
431	139	504	212	568	285	722	358	66
67	432	140	496	213	569	286	723	359
360	68	424	141	497	214	570	287	724

6.

279	716	343	60	416	133	489	206	643
644	271	717	344	61	417	134	490	207
199	645	272	718	345	62	418	135	491
492	200	646	273	719	346	63	419	127
128	493	201	647	274	720	347	55	420
421	129	494	202	648	275	712	348	56
57	422	130	495	203	640	276	713	349
350	58	423	131	487	204	641	277	714
715	351	59	415	132	488	205	642	278

7.

634	270	707	334	51	407	124	561	197
198	635	262	708	335	52	408	125	562
563	190	636	263	709	336	53	409	126
118	564	191	637	264	710	337	54	410
411	119	565	192	638	265	711	338	46
47	412	120	566	193	639	266	703	339
340	48	413	121	567	194	631	267	704
705	341	49	414	122	559	195	632	268
269	706	342	50	406	123	560	196	633

8.

188	625	261	698	325	42	479	115	552
553	189	626	253	699	326	43	480	116
117	554	181	627	254	700	327	44	481
482	109	555	182	628	255	701	328	45
37	483	110	556	183	629	256	702	329
330	38	484	111	557	184	630	257	694
695	331	39	485	112	558	185	622	258
259	696	332	40	486	113	550	186	623
624	260	697	333	41	478	114	551	187

Bottom Layer.

EXAMPLES OF OTHER MAGIC SQUARES BASED ON THE CUBE OF NINE SQUARES

178	615	251	688	405	32	469	105	542
533	169	606	323	679	396	23	461	96
87	524	241	597	314	670	387	14	451
442	159	515	232	588	305	661	378	5
77	433	150	506	223	579	296	652	369
360	68	424	141	497	214	570	287	725
715	351	59	415	132	488	205	642	278
269	706	342	50	406	123	560	196	633
624	260	697	333	41	478	114	551	187

The Front Face A.

543	107	472	36	401	685	249	614	178
97	462	26	391	684	320	604	168	533
452	16	381	674	310	603	239	523	87
6	371	664	300	593	229	522	158	442
361	654	290	583	219	512	148	441	77
725	280	573	209	502	138	431	67	360
279	644	199	492	128	421	57	350	715
634	198	563	118	411	47	340	705	269
188	553	117	482	37	330	695	259	624

The Left Hand Slice B.

How Magic Squares A and B relate to the Cube of Nine Squares. A further Nine Magic Squares can be made in every orthogonal direction.

The Left Hand Slice B.

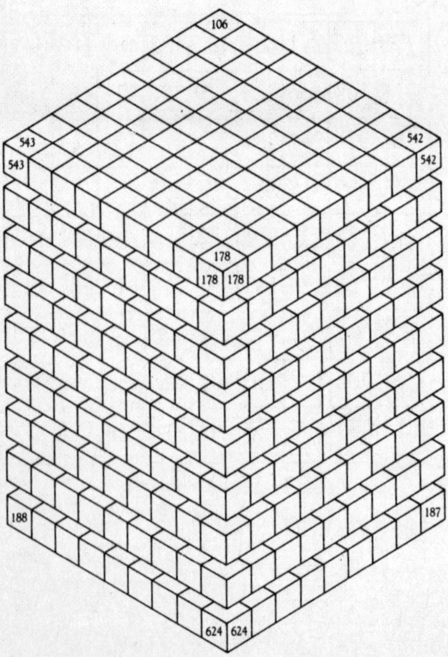

The Front Face A.

Chronology

Fu Hsi (Legendary emperor) .... (Supposedly) 2852 BC
Huang Ti (The Yellow Emperor) .... ca 2697 BC
Oracle bones .... ca 1600 BC

CHOU Dynasty .... 1122-255 BC
Wen Wang .... 1231-1135 BC
Wu Wang .... 1169-1116 BC
Confucius .... 551-479 BC
I Ching .... not before Confucius

CHIN Dynasty .... 255-209 BC
'Burning of the Books' .... 213 BC

WESTERN HAN Dynasty .... 206 BC-AD 25
Yang Hsiung .... 53 BC-AD 18

EASTERN HAN Dynasty .... AD 25-AD 220
Pan Ku .... AD 32-AD 92

SUNG Dynasty .... AD 960-AD 1297
Ssu Ma Kuang .... AD 1019-AD 1086

MING Dynasty .... AD 1368-AD 1628
Ch'en Jen Hsi .... AD 1579-AD 1634

THE SHOU TABULATED

Nov 11	Oct 2	Aug 22	Jul 13	Jun 2	Apr 22	Mar 13	Jan 31	Dec 22
9 成 649 CH'ENG COMPLETING 73	8 沈 568 CH'EN SINKING 64	7 減 487 CHIEN DIMINISHING 55	6 廓 406 K'UO EXTENDING 46	5 睟 325 TSUI YEAR 37	4 更 244 KENG CHANGE 28	3 從 163 TS'UNG COMPLIANCE 19	2 羨 82 HSIEN PRAISE 10	1 中 1 CHUNG CENTRE 1
9 闞 658 CHIH WILL 74	8 內 577 NEI WITHIN 65	7 唫 496 YIN HUMMING 56	6 文 415 WEN LITERATURE 47	5 盛 334 SHENG ABUNDANCE 38	4 斷 253 TUAN SEVERING 29	3 進 172 CHIN ADVANCING 20	2 差 91 CH'A MISTAKE 11	1 周 10 CHOU SURROUNDING 2
9 失 667 SHIH ERROR 75	8 去 586 CH'Ü DEPARTING 66	7 守 505 SHOU PROTECTION 57	6 禮 424 LI PROPRIETY 48	5 居 343 CHÜ DWELLING 39	4 毅 262 I FORTITUDE 30	3 釋 181 SHIH RELEASE 21	2 童 100 T'UNG YOUNG BOY 12	1 礥 19 HSIEN SLOWLY 3
9 劇 676 CHÜ TROUBLES 76	8 晦 595 HUI OBSCURE 67	7 翕 514 HSI RE-UNITING 58	6 逃 433 T'AO ESCAPE 49	5 法 352 FA LAW 40	4 裝 271 CHUANG PRETENCE 31	3 格 190 KE PATTERN 22	2 增 109 TSENG INCREASE 13	1 閑 28 HSIEN BARRIER 4

9 685 馴 *HSÜN* DOMESTICATED 77	8 604 瞢 *MENG* DIMMED 68	7 523 聚 *CHÜ* ASSEMBLY 59	6 442 唐 *T'ANG* DODDER 50	5 361 應 *YING* BEFITTING 41	4 280 衆 *CHUNG* MULTITUDE 32	3 199 夷 *I* HARM 23	2 118 銳 *JUI* SHARPNESS 14	1 37 少 *SHAO* LEAST 5
9 695 將 *CHIANG* TAKING 78	8 613 窮 *CH'IUNG* POVERTY 69	7 532 積 *CHI* STORE 60	6 451 常 *CH'ANG* RULE 51	5 370 迎 *YING* GREETING 42	4 289 密 *MI* INTIMACY 33	3 208 樂 *LO* JOY 24	2 127 達 *TA* PERCEIVING 15	1 46 戾 *LI* TRIBULATION 6
9 703 難 *NAN* DIFFICULTIES 79	8 622 割 *KO* HACKING 70	7 541 飾 *SHIH* ADORN 61	6 460 度 *TU* DEGREE 52	5 379 遇 *YÜ* MEETING 43	4 298 親 *CH'IN* RELATIVES 34	3 217 爭 *CHENG* CONTENTION 25	2 136 交 *CHIAO* EXCHANGE 16	1 55 上 *SHANG* ASCENT 7
9 712 勤 *CH'IN* DILIGENT 80	8 631 止 *CHIH* STOP 71	7 550 疑 *I* DOUBT 62	6 469 永 *YUNG* ETERNITY 53	5 388 竈 *TSAO* STOVE 44	4 307 斂 *LIEN* ACCUMULATION 35	3 226 務 *WU* SCRUTINY 26	2 145 耎 *JUAN* SOFTNESS 17	1 64 干 *KAN (CH'IEN)* OPPOSE (THOUSAND) 8
9 721 養 *YANG* NOURISHING 81	8 640 堅 *CHIEN* OBDURACY 72	7 559 視 *SHIH* INSPECT 63	6 478 昆 *K'UN* POSTERITY 54	5 397 大 *TA* GREAT 45	4 316 疆 *CHIANG* BOUNDARY 36	3 235 事 *SHIH* TRANSACTIONS 27	2 154 傒 *HSI* WAITING 18	1 73 狩 *SHU* PENETRATING 9

The Magic Squares of Master Tsan

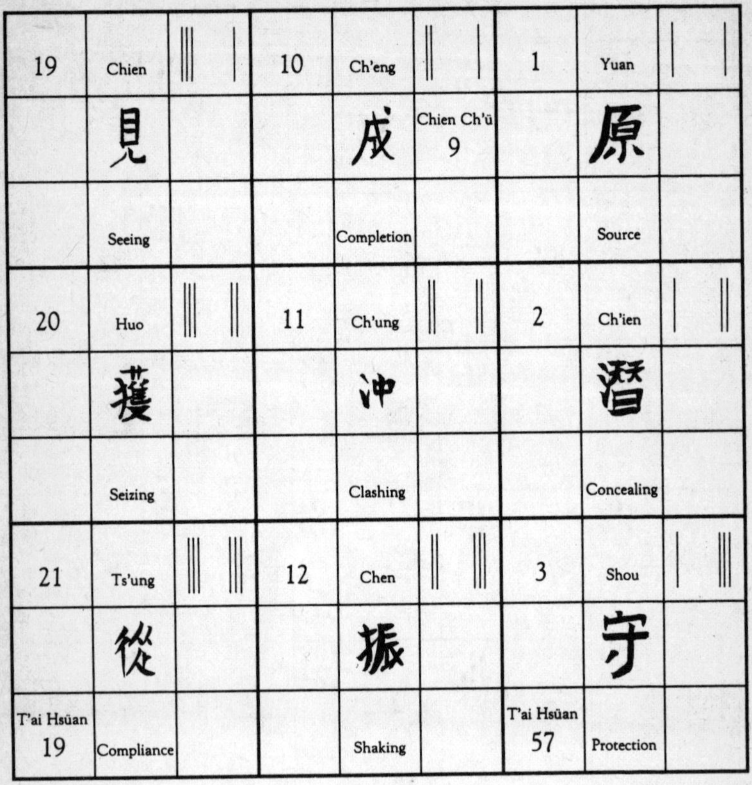

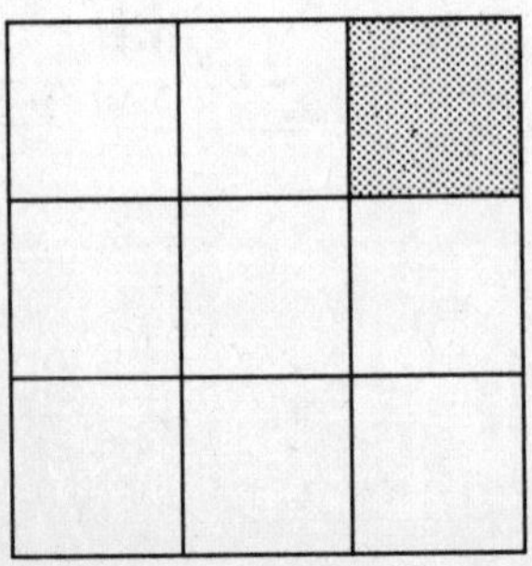

<table>
<tr><td>22</td><td>Chiao</td><td>||| ||||</td><td>13</td><td>Ch'i</td><td>|| ||||</td><td>4</td><td>Hsin</td><td>| ||||</td></tr>
<tr><td></td><td>交</td><td></td><td></td><td>祈</td><td></td><td></td><td>信</td><td></td></tr>
<tr><td>T'ai Hsüan 16</td><td>Exchange</td><td></td><td></td><td>Petition</td><td></td><td></td><td>Trust</td><td></td></tr>
<tr><td>23</td><td>Yü</td><td>||| |||||</td><td>14</td><td>Ch'ang</td><td>|| |||||</td><td>5</td><td>Chih</td><td>| |||||</td></tr>
<tr><td></td><td>育</td><td></td><td></td><td>常</td><td></td><td></td><td>直</td><td></td></tr>
<tr><td></td><td>Nourish</td><td></td><td>T'ai Hsüan 51</td><td>Rule</td><td></td><td></td><td>Upright</td><td></td></tr>
<tr><td>24</td><td>Chuang</td><td>||| ⊤</td><td>15</td><td>Mao</td><td>|| ⊤</td><td>6</td><td>Meng</td><td>| ⊤</td></tr>
<tr><td></td><td>壯</td><td></td><td></td><td>矛</td><td></td><td></td><td>蒙</td><td></td></tr>
<tr><td></td><td>Flourish</td><td>I Ching 34</td><td></td><td>Lance</td><td></td><td></td><td>Obscure</td><td>I Ching 4</td></tr>
</table>

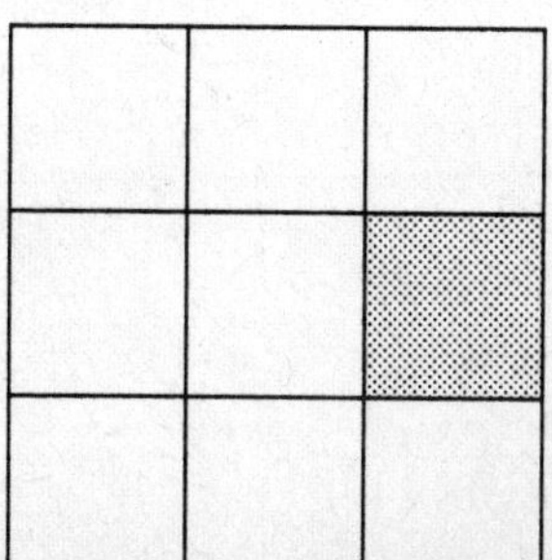

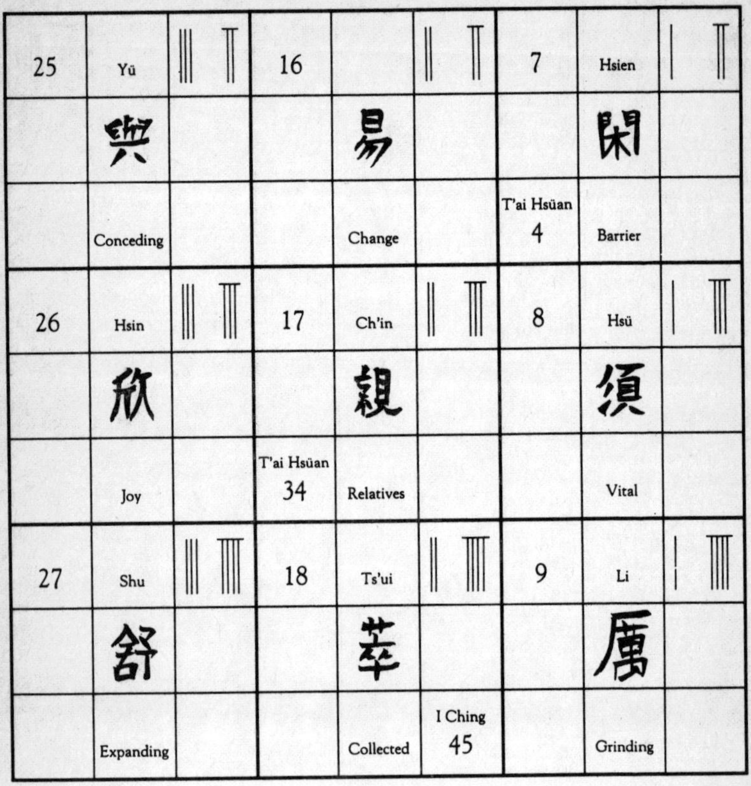
25
Yü
與
Conceding
16
易
Change
7
Hsien
閑
T'ai Hsüan 4
Barrier
26
Hsin
欣
Joy
17
Ch'in
親
T'ai Hsüan 34
Relatives
8
Hsü
須
Vital
27
Shu
舒
Expanding
18
Ts'ui
萃
Collected
I Ching 45
9
Li
厲
Grinding

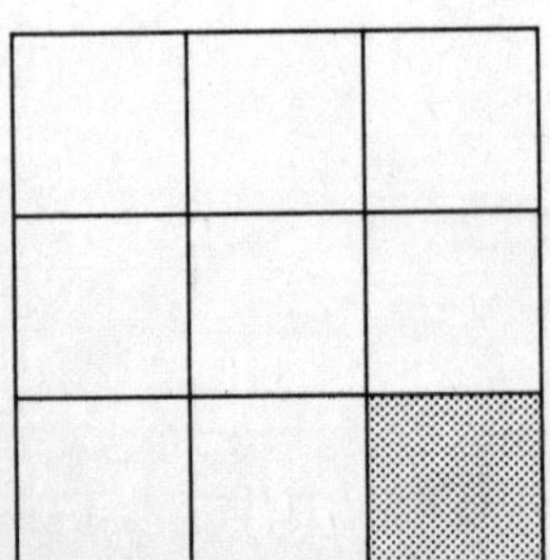

46	Shih	T |	37			28	Pi	|||| |
	飾						比	
T'ai Hsüan 61	Adorn						Comparison	I Ching 8
47	Li	T ||	38			29	K'ai	|||| ||
	戾						開	Chien Ch'ú 11
T'ai Hsüan 6	Violence						Opening	
48	Hsin	T |||	39			30	Chin	|||| |||
Lunar Mansion 11	虛						晉	
	Void						Increase	I Ching 35

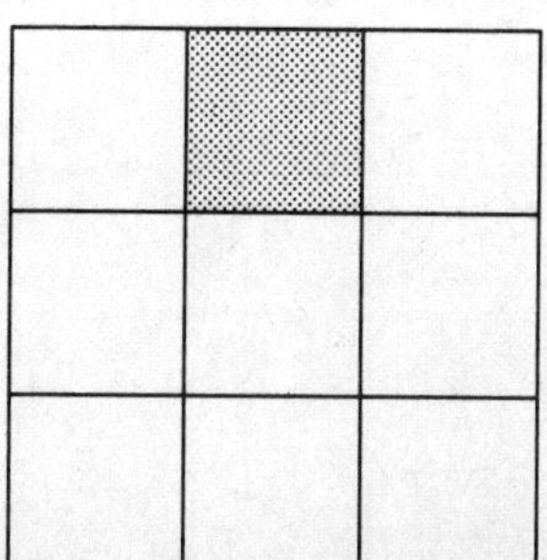

49	Mei	𝍥 𝍣	40			31	Kung	𝍣 𝍣
	昧						公	
	Suppress						Duke	
50	Sun	𝍥 𝍤	41			32	I	𝍣 𝍤
	損						益	
	Injury	I Ching 41					Advantage	I Ching 42
51	Yung	𝍥 𝍥	42			33	Chang	𝍣 𝍥
	用						章	
	Use						Document	

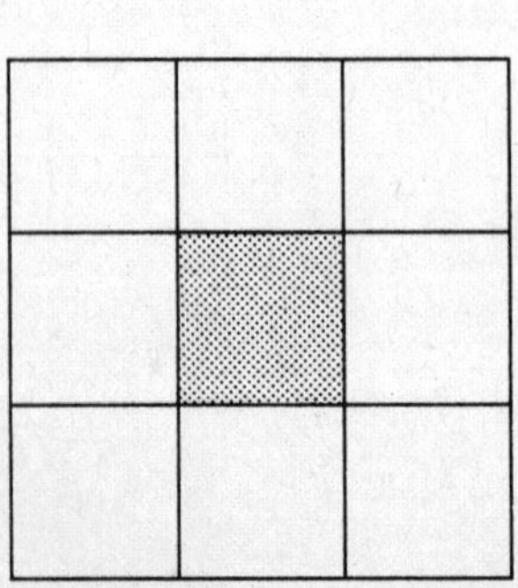

52	Ch'ueh	𝍥 𝍦	43			34	Ying	𝍣 𝍦
	卻						盈	
	Rejection						Overflowing	
53	Weng	𝍥 𝍧	44			35		
	翁							
	Respect							
54	Yuan	𝍥 𝍨	45	Kua	𝍤 𝍨	36		
	遠			寡				
	Remote			Meagre				

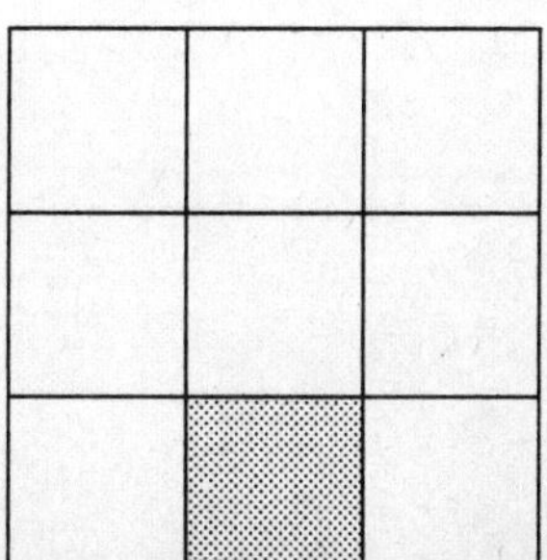

73	Yang	𝍨 𝍠	64	K'uan	𝍧 𝍠	55	Hsing	𝍥 𝍠
	養			寬			迅	
T'ai Hsüan 81	Nourish			Spacious			Swift	
74	Yü	𝍨 𝍡	65	Pin	𝍧 𝍡	56	Chü	𝍥 𝍡
	遇			賓			懼	
T'ai Hsüan 43	Meeting			Guest			Fear	
75	Sheng	𝍨 𝍢	66	Wei	𝍧 𝍢	57	Ch'u	𝍥 𝍢
	勝		Lunar Mansion 12	危	Chien Ch'ü 8		除	
	Vanquish			Danger			Erasing	

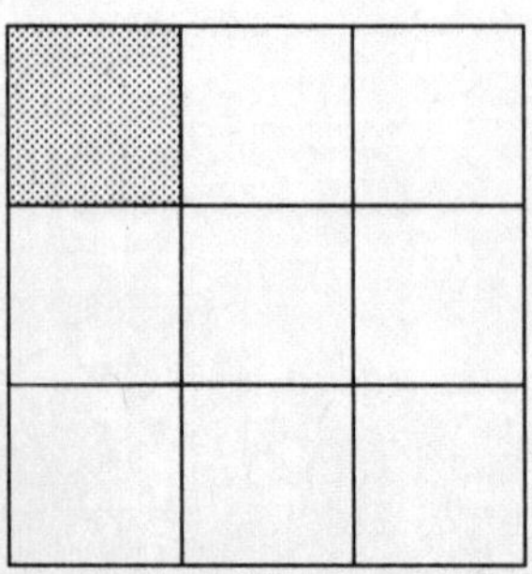

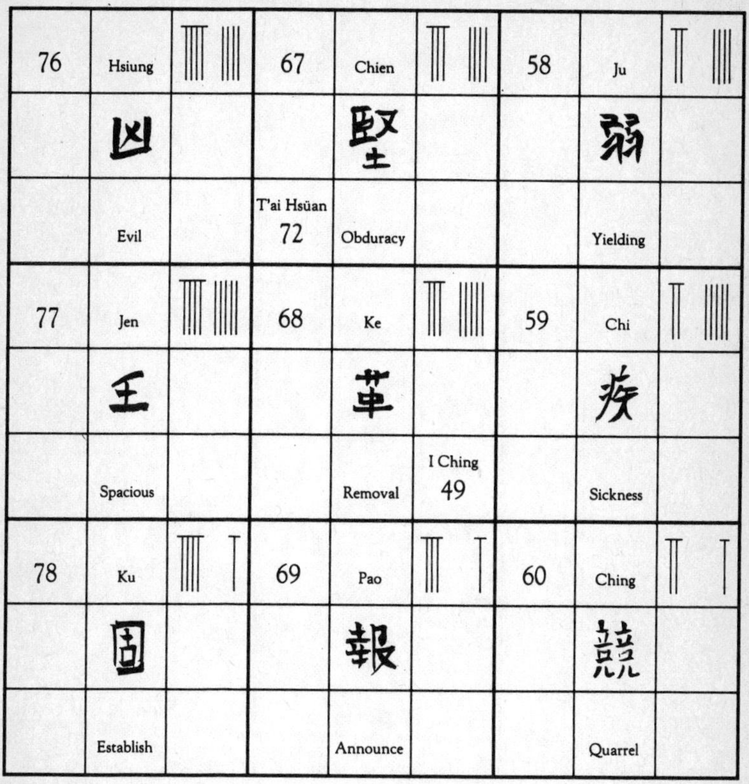
76
Hsiung
凶
Evil
67
Chien
堅
T'ai Hsüan
72
Obduracy
58
Ju
弱
Yielding
77
Jen
壬
Spacious
68
Ke
革
Removal
I Ching
49
59
Chi
疾
Sickness
78
Ku
固
Establish
69
Pao
報
Announce
60
Ching
競
Quarrel

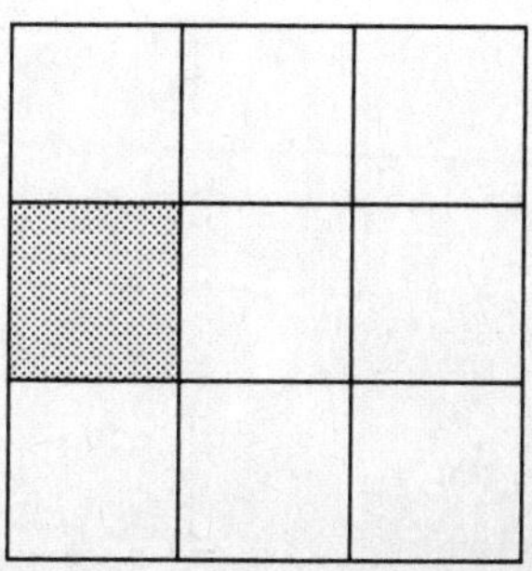

79	I		70	Chi		61	Fen	
	移			止			分	
	Convey		T'ai Hsüan 71	Stop			Division	
80	Sui		71	Jung		62	Sung	
	隨			戎			訟	
	Escort	I Ching 17		Weapons			Litigation	I Ching 6
81	Chung		72	Chieh		63	Shou	
	終			結			收	Chien Ch'ü 10
	End			Contract			Receive	

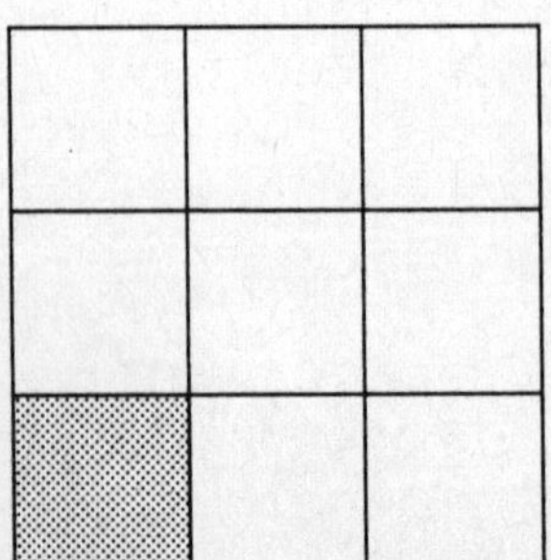

BIBLIOGRAPHY

Chatley, H. Chinese Natural Philosophy and Magic. *Journal of the Royal Society of Arts*, Vol LIX, 1911.

Confucius. *Lun Yü* (Analects).

Couling, S. *Encyclopaedia Sinica*, Kelly and Walsh, Shanghai, 1917.

Courant, R., and Robbins, H. *What is Mathematics?*, OUP, 1941.

Daily Telegraph. Science Report, Letters, 14.6.82.

Deacon, R. *The Book of Fate; its origins and uses*, Frederick Muller, London.

Diem, K. and Lentner, C. *Scientific Tables*. Geigy, Macclesfield.

Feng Yu Lan. *A History of Chinese Philosophy, Vol. 2*, Princeton University Press, 1953.

Giles, H. A. *A Chinese Biographical Dictionary*, Reprinted by Ch'eng Wen Publishing Co., Taipei.

Giles, H. A. *Chinese English Dictionary*, 1st and 2nd Editions.

Harvard Yenching Institute *Sinological Index Series* supplement No. 10. A Concordance to the I Ching. Reprint by Ch'eng Wen, Taipei.

Hoang (Huang) P. le P. *Catalogue des eclipses . . . dans les documents chinoises*. Varietes sinologiques, No. 56.

Hofstadter, D. R. *Gödel-Escher-Bach: An Eternal Golden Braid*. Penguin, 1979.

Hsü Ch'in T'ing. *I Ching Yen Chiu* (I Ching Researches). Wu Chow.

Hughes, E. R. *Chinese Philosophy in Classical Times*. 'Everyman' series. Dent and Sons, London, 1937.

K'ang Hsi Tzu Tien (Emperor K'ang Hsi) (attrib) *Imperial Dictionary*. 1716.

K'ao Ku. (*Kaogu*). (*Archaeology*). 1981, Vol. 2.

K'ao Ku Hsüeh Pao. (*Kaogu Xuebao*). (*Acta Archaeologica Sinica*). 1980, No. 4.

Karlgren, B. *Grammata Serica Recensa*. Bulletin of the Museum of Far Eastern Antiquities, Stockholm, 1972.

Li Hsüeh Ch'in (Li Xueqin). *The Wonder of Chinese Bronzes*. Foreign Languages Press, Peking, 1980.

Ling Ch'i Ching (The Spirit Chess Classic) Tao T'sang; Wieger 285. Also see Tung Fang Shuo.

Loewe, Michael. *Ancient Cosmologies*, Allen and Unwin.

Loewe, Michael. *The Manuscripts from Tomb Number Three, Ma Wang Tui*. Proceedings of the International Conference on Sinology, 1980.

Loewe, Michael. *Ways to Paradise*, Allen and Unwin.

Loewe, Michael, and Blacker, Carmen, (editors). *Divination and Oracles*, Allen and Unwin.

Mayers, W. F. *Chinese Reader's Manual*, American Presbyterian Mission Press, 1874.

Needham, Joseph. *Science and Civilisation in China*, (Particularly Volume 2, 'The History of Scientific Thought'), Cambridge University Press.

v. Oppolzer, T. *Canon der Finsternisse*, Vienna, 1887.

Schindler, B. *Inscriptions on Ancient Chinese Bronzes*, Ostasiatische Zeitschrift, 1915, Vol. 3.

Schlagintweit, Emil. *Buddhism in Tibet*. London, 1863.

Schönberg, Arnold. *Structural Functions of Harmony*, (ed. Humphrey Searle), Williams and Norgate, 1954.

Science Foundation Course Team: *The Nucleus of the Atom*, Open University Press.

Shchutskii, I. K. *Researches on the I Ching*, trs Wm. L. Macdonald, Tsuyoshi Hasegawa and Hellmut Wilhelm, Routledge and Kegan Paul, 1979.

Shchutskii, I. K. *The Chinese Classic — 'the Book of Changes'* (In Russian),Izdatelstvo Vostochnoy Litiraturi, Moscow, 1960.

Sherrill, W. A., and Chu, W. K. *Anthology of the I Ching*, Routledge and Kegan Paul.

Shun Chen Tang. (Perfection of Goodness College). *K'uei Pi I Ching*, Late Ch'ing.

Sung, Z. D. *The Text of the I Ching* (In Chinese, with Legge's translation), Wen Hua, Shanghai, 1935.

Times, The. Science Reports: 25.1.83, 26.1.83.

Tung Fang Shuo (attrib). *Ling Ch'i Ching* (Spirit Chess Classic), Shang Wu Yin Shu Kuan, Shanghai 1936. Also see 'Ling Ch'i Ching'.

Wilhelm, Hellmut. *Die Wandlung. Acht Vorträge zum I-Ging*. Vetch, Peiping, 1944.

Wylie, A. *Eclipses recorded in Chinese works*. Chinese Researches, Shanghai, 1898.

Yang Hsiung. *T'ai Hsüan Ching*. Edited by Ch'en Jen Hsi, 1632, British Library Department of Oriental Manuscripts and Printed Books, 15323 b16/2.

Yang Hsiung. *T'ai Hsüan Ching*, Commentary by Ssu Ma Kuang, 1898.

Yang Hsiung. *T'ai Hsüan Ching*, Commentary by Ssu Ma Kuang, Ssu Pu Pei Yao, Shanghai, 1927-36.

Yang Hsiung. *T'ai Hsüan Ching*, Commentary by Fan Wang, appendix by Wang Lai, and philological notes by Lin Yü. Facsimile of Ming reproduction of Sung copy. Ssu Pu Ts'ung K'an No. 80. Commercial Press, Shanghai. (Several different editions on different sizes of paper.)

Yang Hsiung. *T'ai Yuan Ching* (=T'ai Hsüan Ching, but avoiding the taboo of the name of Hsüan Ti), Ts'ung Wen Shu Chu, 1874.

The illustrations are taken from the *Ch'in Ting Shu Ching T'u Shuo*, the Imperial Illustrated Edition of the Shu Ching (Historical Classic) 1905.

ACKNOWLEDGEMENTS

I would like to express my grateful thanks to the staff of the British Library's Department of Oriental Manuscripts and Printed Books, who at all levels have been considerate and helpful, not only for the expertise of Mr H. H. Nelson and Beth McKillip, but also for the warm and friendly assistance of the counter staff, and the uncomplaining porters who on more than one memorable occasion have carried, armful by armful, several hundred volumes from a complete collection of classical works so that I could identify a reference. I must also acknowledge the help given by Dr Richard Pankhurst, of the Royal Asiatic Society's library, and important assistance provided by the staff at the library of the School of Oriental and African Studies, London.

The library staff of the Royal Astronomical Society provided me with vital data on eclipses. Dr Michael Loewe, of Cambridge University, has been of greater assistance than he could possibly know, and I am also indebted to Dr Anneliese Bulling, and Dr Burchard Mansvelt Beck, for important clues.

Thanks too, are due to my friend Gwyn Woolcock for encouragement when it was most needed, and to Lester Hagen for artistic and administrative help.

Finally, this book would still not have seen the light of day were it not for the foresight of Michael Cox of Aquarian Press, and its indefatigable editor, Simon Franklin.

GENERAL INDEX